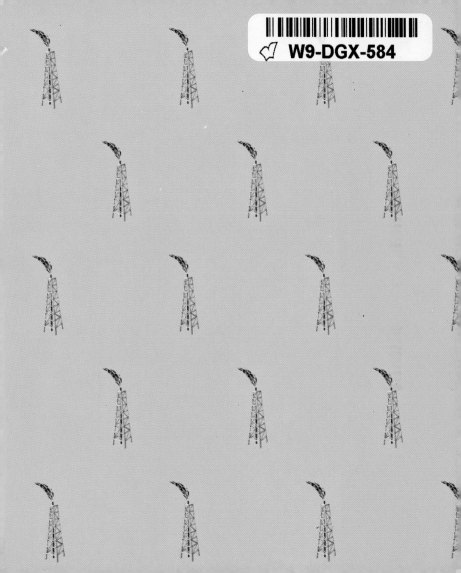

W9-DGX-584

OKLAHOMA

ART OF THE STATE

ART OF THE STATE

OKLAHOMA

The Spirit of America

Text by Barbara Palmer

Harry N. Abrams, Inc., Publishers

NEW YORK

This book was prepared for publication at
Walking Stick Press, San Francisco

Project staff:
    Series Designer: Linda Herman
    Series Editor: Diana Landau

For Harry N. Abrams, Inc.:
    Series Editor: Ruth A. Peltason

Page 1: In the current version of the famed Pawnee Bill Wild West Show, Wayne McCombs portrays Pawnee Bill and rides the trademark Appaloosa horse. *Photo David Crenshaw*

Page 2: Traditional beaded cloth shoulder bag by Jay McGirt (Eucha), used as powwow regalia. *Photo David Crenshaw*

Library of Congress Cataloging-in-Publication Data

Palmer, Barbara.
    Oklahoma : the spirit of America, state by state / by Barbara Palmer.
        p.   cm. — (Art of the state)
    Includes bibliographical references and index.
    ISBN 0–8109–5563–6
    1. Oklahoma—Civilization—Pictorial works.   2. Oklahoma —
Miscellanea.   I. Title.   II. Series.
F695.P35   1999
976.6—dc21   98–43098

Harry N. Abrams, Inc.
100 Fifth Avenue
New York, N.Y. 10011
www.abramsbooks.com

The Scarlet Heaven by Poteet Victory, 1996. Of Choctaw and Cherokee descent, Victory grew up in Idabel, in the Choctaw Nation. Classically trained in painting, he creates both landscapes like this Oklahoma scene and abstract works based on tribal symbolism. *Poteet Victory Gallery, Santa Fe*

CONTENTS

> *"We know we belong to the land,*
> *And the land we belong to is grand!"*
>
> Richard Rodgers and Oscar Hammerstein II, from Oklahoma!

Home to more Native Americans than any other state, Oklahoma could thereby lay claim to being the most truly American place. But more than this, the great themes of our national story are reflected in the state's history and geography. Native America, the American West, and the American Dream all come together under Oklahoma's big skies—sometimes meeting in one person, like Cherokee humorist and rope spinner Will Rogers or Chiricahua Apache sculptor Allan Houser. The first of Geronimo's band to be born after their release from Fort Sill, Houser lived to see his work gracing the White House lawn.

Art and religious tradition colored the daily lives of Oklahoma's earliest people: the Mound Builders in the eastern hills, the Wichita bands that farmed the river valleys, the Caddos in the southern pine forests, and the fearsome Plains tribes, following the buffalo over the grassland. The 19th-century diaspora of Native tribes from other parts of the United States brought new languages, ceremonies, and aesthetics to Oklahoma. Osage lullabies, Cherokee flute songs, Ponca drumbeats, and dozens more sounds mingled in what came to be called Indian Territory. Its citizens lived the breadth of American experience, sweet and bitter, alongside the rest of the nation, hewing logs for cabins, planting crops, then taking up arms against their tribal countryfolk in the Civil War.

Oklahoma had a big hand in creating that quintessential American

Provisions by Brenda Kennedy Grummer, 1976. *Philbrook Museum of Art, Tulsa*

hero, the cowboy. The Chisholm Trail ran through the heart of Indian Territory, carrying millions of head of cattle to the rich grass of the Cherokee Outlet. The culture born then lives on today, in handshake deals, small-town rodeos, and a stubborn love of hard work and horses. It lingers, too, in the national imagination, thanks to beloved performing cowboys like Rogers and native son Gene Autry. Oklahoma's cowboy poets crystallize the

West into a few pithy lines, and Oklahoma voices—like Garth Brooks, Reba McEntire, and Vince Gill—have helped define American country music.

Settlement came to most of the state not as an orderly march, but in a deluge. A series of land runs drew thousands from all over the country, the desperate and the visionary, filling Oklahoma's chronicle with more than its share of scoundrels and saints. The settlers brought along their own music, customs, and dreams to sustain them as they went about planting wheat and cotton and building churches and schools. Their humor and resolve shaped the characters in Lynn Riggs's play *Green Grow the Lilacs,* adapted into the high-spirited musical *Oklahoma!* The heroes of Edna Ferber's novel *Cimarron* only seemed larger than life: Ferber drew her characters straight from Oklahoma Territory, the men and women who built a state in a single generation.

Money, too, came in torrents, as oil burst from the ground and rained down by the barrelful. At the turn of the last century, Tulsa was a sleepy cross-roads known as "Tulsey Town." Scarcely three decades later, it was crowned the "Oil Capital of the World" and boasted Art Deco skyscrapers and man-sions modeled on European castles. Oil fortunes enabled Oklahomans to buy the best, and they did—an office building designed by Frank Lloyd Wright, Renaissance paintings, gold leaf ceilings. But the oil barons invested, too, in art that was of their place. Thomas Gilcrease assembled a renowned collection of Western art and Native American paintings, sculpture, and regalia, and bequeathed the Gilcrease Museum of Art to Tulsa. Philbrook Museum, founded by oilman Waite Phillips, acquired medieval art but also nurtured a new genre with an annual Native American painting competition.

Oklahoma's diverse strains have compounded into a wholly original essence. It sounds in the soaring improvisations of jazz pioneer Charlie

Flight of Spirit, mural by Mike Larsen in the Oklahoma State Capitol, dedicated 1991. Oklahoma's five Indian prima ballerinas were designated in 1997 as state treasures. *Courtesy the artist and the Oklahoma Arts Council*

Christian, the folksongs of Woody Guthrie, the measured prose of Ralph Ellison, and the lyricism of Cheyenne poet Lance Henson. It's heard in the rhythms of powwow drums, keeping time with the cicadas in the summer twilight, and in ragtime pianos joining pioneer fiddles to create Western swing. The visual arts, too, share a heritage of old forms giving birth to new ones. Native American artists transfer their symbolic language of shape and color from buffalo hide to canvas and stone, while Oklahoma writers preserve the cadences of storytellers in poems and novels drawn from a deep well of human experience.

Oklahoma is a young state, its 2007 centennial just appearing on the horizon at this writing. Oklahoma's frontier—energetic, raucous, and full of contradictions—has vanished so recently that an afterimage still burns. With the past and future both close at hand, Oklahoma artists are just hitting their stride. ♠

OKLAHOMA

"The Sooner State"
46th State

Date of Statehood
NOVEMBER 16, 1907

Capital
OKLAHOMA CITY

Bird
SCISSOR-TAILED
FLYCATCHER

Wildflower
INDIAN BLANKET

Tree
REDBUD

Animal
BISON, OR BUFFALO

Rock
ROSE ROCK

Oklahoma's official emblems are an amalgam of Native American and frontier images, creating a common vision in a state that's been both a place of exile and a promised land. The state tree, the redbud—chosen for the way it cheered homesteaders breaking sod on the plains—puts down roots alongside the state wildflower, the hardy Indian blanket. The state's first flag, a field with 46 stars, was replaced by one featuring an Osage warrior's buckskin shield, crossed by two signs of peace: an Indian pipe and an olive branch. From the lively scissor-tailed flycatcher and the majestic buffalo that again roams the prairie, to its rousing state song, Oklahoma's symbols reflect its defining qualities: energy and optimism. Throughout its colorful history, Oklahoma has met every challenge by embracing the motto "Labor Conquers All." ♠

Scissor-tailed
flycatcher
and mistletoe

"Labor Conquers All"

State motto

"Oklahoma!"

In 1953, "Oklahoma!"—the signature song of Broadway's first modern musical—became the state's official song, replacing a staid anthem, "Oklahoma: A Toast," and quickly topping the charts as the most hummable state song. The Rodgers and Hammerstein musical was based on Claremore writer Lynn Riggs's play *Green Grow the Lilacs.*

Oklahoma, where the wind comes sweepin' down the plain
(And the wavin' wheat can sure smell sweet
When the wind comes right behind the rain)
Oklahoma! Every night my honey lamb and I
Sit alone and talk and watch a hawk
Makin' lazy circles in the sky.
We know we belong to the land
And the land we belong to is grand.
And when we say:
"Ee-ee-ow! A-yip-i-o-ee-ay!"
We're only sayin' You're doin' fine, Oklahoma!
Oklahoma, O.K!

*Words by Oscar Hammerstein II,
music by Richard Rodgers*

Above: Oklahoma! postage stamp. *Below:* "Miss Oklahoma" carving by Earl Eyman of Drumright, c. 1930s. *America Hurrah Archive, New York*

Opposite below: Indian blanket, the state wildflower, is better known than the official flower, the nonnative mistletoe. *Photo Harvey Payne.* The name "Oklahoma" comes from two Choctaw words: *okla,* which means "people," and *hum,* meaning "red." It was first proposed as the name for a new Native American territory or state.

Aunt Bill's Brown Candy

A cross between a praline and divinity, this uses pecans harvested from the state's abundant groves. It was popularized by an Oklahoma City newspaper columnist; the origin of "Aunt Bill" is a mystery.

6 cups white sugar
2 cups cream or whole milk
¼ tsp. baking soda
½ cup butter
1 tsp. vanilla
4 cups pecans, broken

Pour 2 cups sugar into a heavy iron skillet; place over low heat. Stir with wooden spoon (about 20 minutes; mixture should look like light brown syrup). Mix remaining sugar with 2 cups cream or milk in a heavy kettle; cook slowly to a boil over low heat. As soon as sugar is melted, begin pouring it in a very fine stream into the milk mixture, keeping heat very low; stir constantly. Cook and stir until mixture reaches 238 to 240° F, nearly to hard-ball stage. Immediately add soda, then butter, stirring until melted. Cool 20 minutes. Add vanilla; beat until thick and dull. Add pecans. Turn into buttered pans; cool before cutting.

A Rock by Any Other Name

Rose rock, the state mineral, isn't really a rock at all, but a barite crystal, formed from barium sulfate and sand when the prehistoric Permian Sea evaporated. Reddish iron oxide in the soil gives the formations a roselike glow. Most rose rocks are found in a

Barite, or rose rock

band across the central part of the state, but the poetic tale of their origin comes from the Cherokee tribe in eastern Oklahoma: along the Trail of Tears, a warrior gave his beloved a wild rose. The two became separated along the way and as the grieving Cherokee maiden walked on, carrying all her belongings, her tears mixed with blood from her chafed hands. Wherever her tears fell, they made the shape of a rose.

Left: The Oklahoma State Capitol in Oklahoma City was designed by Solomon Layton and built in 1914–17. *Photo Kent and Donna Dannen. Opposite:* Oklahoma's state seal, depicted in stained glass on the ceiling of the capitol, incorporates emblems of the Union along with those of five Indian nations resettled here: the Cherokee, Chickasaw, Creek, Choctaw, and Seminole. *Photo Tim Thompson*

They Came "Sooner"

Between 1889 and 1895, as hundreds of thousands of acres were opened to non-Indian settlement in six land runs, the odds were usually against the would-be settlers. Some homesteaders couldn't resist the temptation to sneak across the borders a little "sooner" than the law allowed, employing such subterfuge as soaping their horses to make them look lathered from exertion. It's estimated that during a run into Oklahoma Territory in 1895, fully half of the claimants were "Sooners." In 1901, when the Kiowa–Comanche lands

were opened, the federal government switched to a lottery.

Above: Engraving of an Oklahoma land run, c. 1880s. *San Francisco Public Library. Below:* Buffalo Bull by W. R. Leigh, 1911. Born in West Virginia, Leigh made the first of many trips into the West in 1906. *Gilcrease Museum, Tulsa*

The herds of bison (also correctly called "buffalo") that once grazed Oklahoma's prairies were so numerous that the paths they wore in the land were almost as conspicuous as roads. Prized for their hides and tongues, bison were hunted to the brink of extinction after the Civil War. In 1907, preservationists brought a herd of 15 by rail from a New York zoo to the Wichita Mountains Wildlife Refuge. The bison population at the refuge is maintained at about 500 animals; 300 more graze in the Tallgrass Prairie Preserve.

c. A.D. 800 Religious center of Mound Builders civilization.

1541 Coronado crosses western Oklahoma, looking for the Seven Cities of Cibola.

1719 French trader Bernard de La Harpe makes trading alliances with Caddoan tribes.

1786 Wichita village on the Red River is a trading hub, dealing in furs and goods.

1803 United States purchases Louisiana, including Oklahoma, from France.

1805 The Kiowa move from the northern plains to Oklahoma.

1820 The Osage Union Mission is established by Presbyterian missionaries.

1824 Fort Gibson established on the Arkansas River.

1830 President Andrew Jackson signs the Indian Removal Act, creates Indian Territory.

1830 Choctaw Tribe begins removal to Indian Territory.

1836 Treaty compels Cherokee to exchange lands in Georgia for Indian Territory lands.

1842 Seminoles relocate to eastern Oklahoma.

1844 *The Cherokee Advocate*, Oklahoma's first newspaper, published in English and Cherokee.

1851 Cherokees open first seminaries for higher learning west of the Mississippi.

1853 Chickasaw build council house in Tishomingo.

1861 Cherokees, Choctaw, Seminoles, Muscogee (Creeks), and Chickasaw ally with the Confederacy.

1863 Native Americans, African Americans, and whites fight side by side at the Civil War Battle of Honey Springs in Rentiesville.

1866 Reconstruction treaties cede tribes' western lands to federal government.

1867 Treaty of Medicine Lodge creates reservations in western Oklahoma for Cheyenne, Arapaho, Kiowa, and Comanche.

1867 Longhorn cattle begin moving north along the Chisholm Trail.

1871 First railroad, Missouri-Kansas-Texas (MKT), built in Oklahoma.

1883 Sun Dance outlawed in Indian Territory.

1889 Central Oklahoma opened to non-Indian settlement during Land Rush.

1890 Organic Act creates Oklahoma Territory.

1893 The Cherokee Outlet opened to non-Indian settlement.

1894 Geronimo and 295 Chiricahua Apache imprisoned at Fort Sill.

1897 First commercial oil well drilled in Bartlesville.

1900 Population 800,000.

1904 The Red Fork oil field is discovered at the Creek settlement Tulsey Town.

1905 Congress rejects a proposal to create a Native American state called "Sequoyah."

1907 Indian Territory and Oklahoma Territory are joined to create Oklahoma, the 46th state; tribal governments are abolished.

1910 State capital moved from Guthrie to Oklahoma City.

1911 Clyde Cessna tests his first airplane on Oklahoma salt plains.

1914 Sculptor Allan Houser is the first Chiracahua Apache child born after tribe's release from Fort Sill.

1923 Osage receive $27 million in payment for oil leases.

1924 Oklahoma City Blue Devils jazz band organized—members would include Lester Young, Jimmy Rushing, and William "Count" Basie.

1926 Highway officials approve creation of Route 66.

1928 Duncan oilman Earl Haliburton establishes Southwest Air Fast Express, later American Airlines.

1928 "Kiowa Five" exhibit opens in Prague.

1930 Population 2,401,000.

1931 First American Indian Exposition held in Anadarko.

1934 Will Rogers is nation's top box-office attraction.

1936 Oklahoma Indian Welfare Act allows tribes to enact new constitutions.

1940 Woody Guthrie writes "This Land Is Your Land."

1943 Broadway musical *Oklahoma!* opens.

1945 Post–Dust Bowl population drops 16 percent to 2,028,000.

1947 Woodward tornado kills 116 people on April 10.

1959 Prohibition repealed in Oklahoma.

1990 Population 3,271,000.

1995 Murrah Federal Building bombed in Oklahoma City, kills 168 people.

1997 Native son Garth Brooks named Country Music Entertainer of the Year for the fourth time.

Winding Stair Mountains, in the game-filled Ouachita National Forest. Ouachita is the French spelling of two Choctaw words, *owa* and *chito,* which together mean "big hunt." *Photo Michael Hardeman*

The Twin Territories

When two frontier territories joined to become Oklahoma, the state's outline was drawn by politics. Had geography been the guide, the map would look different, for western and eastern Oklahoma are distinct right down to their soils. The two regions share the mercurial Red River as a southern border, but little else.

The rusty red earth of western Oklahoma is a prehistoric memento, colored by iron oxide left behind from the evaporating Permian Sea. Although flat, this land is nonetheless geologically intriguing. The red earth rises suddenly in gypsum-striped buttes; canyons and alabaster caverns are pocketed into the prairie. Sand dunes loom 70 feet high, and shorebirds flock to shimmering salt plains. To the southwest rises the blue line of the ancient Wichita Mountains, their boulders worn to sculpture by eons of wind and rain.

The eastern half of the state is a world apart—a sweep of hills blanketed with hickory, oak, and shortleaf pine. The Ozark and the Ouachita Mountains spill over the eastern border, then gradually smooth into limestone bluffs and rolling prairie. With double the rainfall found in the west, eastern Oklahoma's landscape is laced with mountain streams, mineral springs, waterfalls, seeps, bogs, and cypress swamps.

Red Rock Canyon. Western Oklahoma's red rock canyons were formed 200 million years ago, when a prehistoric sea carved 200-feet deep canyons into the sandstone of the Permian Red Beds. *Photo Michael Hardeman*

"WE WERE FOUR DAYS TRAVELING OVER a beautiful country, most of the way prairie, and generally along near the base of a stupendous range of mountains of reddish granite in many places piled up to an immense height without tree or shrubbery on them; looking as if they had actually dropped from the clouds in such a confused mass and all lay where they had fallen."

George Catlin, describing the "Great Camanchee Village" near the north fork of the Red River, in Letters and Notes on…North American Indians, *1841*

An Empire of Grasses

A canopy of trees covered primeval Oklahoma, until the rising Rocky Mountains blocked moisture flowing inward from the Pacific Ocean. As the interior dried, prairie conquered forest in western and central Oklahoma, and a great banner of grass unfurled toward the east. Three distinct types of prairies are found in the state. Farthest west is the drought-resistant short-grass prairie—level land dominated by curly buffalo grass and blue grama grass. Once strewn with wildflowers, it was grazing land for rivers of migrating bison and pronghorn. In central Oklahoma, shortgrass blends with midsized wheatgrass, needlegrass, and little bluestem, creating mixed-grass prairie. Sand and sediment washed down from the Rockies nurture the rich, loosely packed soil of northwestern and central Oklahoma, which produces myriad acres of wheat. Still farther east grow the prairie's glory: the tall grasses. Indian grass, switchgrass, and big bluestem may reach eight feet in the Tallgrass Prairie Preserve, a 37,000-acre remnant of the vast

midwestern prairie. Bison are the high-profile inhabitants, but the preserve also is home to 79 species of mammals and 250 species of birds, including prairie chickens, bald eagles, and short-eared owls.

"THE IMPRESSION WAS ONE OF SPACE; WHISPERING SPACE. The curved blue sky met the undulating emerald on all sides among the rounded hills…it was wild space, yet it was never silent."

John Joseph Mathews, Wah'Kon-Tah: The Osage and the White Man's Road, 1932

Above: Prairie Fire by Francis Blackbear Bosin (Kiowa-Comanche), c. 1953. This painting won the Philbrook Museum's Indian Annual painting competition in 1953. *Philbrook Museum Opposite above:* Compass plant, Gayfeather Tallgrass Prairie. *Photo Harvey Payne. Opposite below:* Blacktail prairie dogs. *Photo Kim Hart*

Crucified Land by Alexander Hogue, 1939. Hogue came to national attention when his stylized paintings documenting the ravages of agricultural overproduction were reproduced in *Life* magazine during the heart of the Depression. *Gilcrease Museum, Tulsa*

Oklahoma's wide plains are a rendezvous for dry cold air from the north and warm, moist air from the Gulf of Mexico, brewing up a spectacular array of abruptly changing weather patterns. The most awesome weather occurs during late spring and early summer, when roiling clouds can quickly build 70,000-foot-high thunderheads. Some spin into tornadoes, unleashing 250- to 300-mph winds. Per square mile, Oklahoma has more violent tornadoes and storms than any other state. ▲

"Dusty Old Dust"

In April 1935, the term "Dust Bowl" entered the American lexicon, coined by an Associated Press reporter filing a report on an ominous dust storm in Cimarron County, in Oklahoma's Panhandle. Two generations of homesteaders had plowed up the thick roots of the shortgrass prairie to make way for wheat and corn; when a sustained drought hit the High Plains in the 1930s, there was nothing to hold the soil. A hundred thousand people left Oklahoma during the "Dirty Thirties," many of them tenant cotton farmers reeling from drops in cotton prices. Other farmers stuck it out and survived.

"THE HARDEST WEATHER IN THE WORLD IS THERE. Winter brings blizzards, hot tornadic winds arise in the spring, and in summer, the prairie is an anvil's edge."

N. Scott Momaday, The Way to Rainy Mountain, *1969*

Above: Production photo from the 1996 movie *Twister.* Much of the film was shot on location in Oklahoma, where scientists indeed "chase" tornadoes in efforts to predict where their wrath will fall. *Photo Shooting Star. Left: Farmer and sons walking in the face of a duststorm, Cimarron County, Oklahoma, 1936.* Arthur Rothstein's photograph, taken for the Farmer's Security Administration, became a national symbol of Dust Bowl desolation. *Corbis-Bettmann*

Right: Reproduction of a Caddo home, Anadarko. *Photo Tim Thompson*
Below: Incised bottle from the Spiro Mounds in southeastern Oklahoma, Mississippian culture. Between A.D. 1150 and 1300, the site was the ceremonial and trade center of an inter-tribal confederation stretching from the Rockies to Virginia and from the Gulf of Mexico to the Great Lakes. Its artifacts show links to pre-Columbian Mexico. *University of Oklahoma Photo Pictures of Record*

Wandering families of big-game hunters were the first humans to leave their mark in Oklahoma. The hunters killed primordial buffalo, mammoth, and camels with spears or stampeded them over cliffs. Projectile points 12,000 years old have been found throughout the state. Oklahoma's first artists of record lived in caves in the Panhandle about 4,000 years ago and painted the walls with animal and human figures. A later group of artists, the Mound Builders, lived in eastern Oklahoma between 2000 B.C. and A.D. 1450. They left behind, near Spiro, 11 earthen mounds containing the cedar log

homes and tombs of priests, filled with quartz and jade, carved wooden masks, stone effigies, baskets, and prehistoric lace. The Mounds culture was mysteriously interrupted in the 13th century, possibly by nomadic tribes hunting game on the western plains.

Trade with Europeans began after 1719, when Bernard de La Harpe established a post among the Caddoan-speaking Wichita—farmers who lived in dome-shaped grass houses along the Red River. La Harpe and the Wichita created the state's first industry: a brisk fur trade, swapping beaver, otter, mink, and muskrat pelts and tanned buffalo hides for French guns and ammunition. The Wichitas' influence declined after 1763, when Spain won control of the land. The territory reverted to France in 1800, destined to be part of the Louisiana Purchase. ♠

Above: Santa Fe Trail artifact from one of the early Spanish expeditions exploring north and east from Mexico. *Photo Bruce Dale/ National Geographic Society. Right:* Naturalist Thomas Nuttall produced the first scientific study of the future state while battling malaria on his travels. He was the stereotypic eccentric botanist; the French keelboatmen who took him down the Mississippi called him "le Fou" (the crazy one).

When the United States acquired the Louisiana Territory from France, neither nation was sure where the boundaries of the new land lay, but soldiers and botanists were eager to take its measure. The U.S. government's first attempt at exploring the Red River was turned back by a column of Spanish cavalry, just inside what is now Oklahoma's southeastern corner. Lieutenant B. Wilkinson, who with five men split off from Zebulon Pike's Colorado expedition in 1807, had better luck entering the territory, but his little band nearly froze to death. In 1819, America and Spain settled on the Red River as the international border, and English botanist Thomas Nuttall traveled through eastern Oklahoma rhapsodizing about the plant and animal life. The first travel essay about Oklahoma was penned in 1832 by Washington Irving, who toured its northeast in the company of soldiers and a Swiss count, looking for the real American West. ♠

"THESE VAST PLAINS, BEAUTIFUL ALMOST AS THE FANCIED elysium, were now splendid (with)... azure Larkspur, gilded Coreopsides, Rudbeckias, fragrant Phloxes, and the purple Psilotria."

Thomas Nuttall, A Journal of Travels into the Arkansas Territory During the Year 1819

U.S. Dragoons Meeting Comanches and Buffalo by George Catlin, c. 1840s. Catlin accompanied the dragoons into Indian Territory in 1833–34; this encounter took place near Fort Gibson on the Arkansas River. *Gilcrease Museum, Tulsa*

By greatly expanding the American frontier, the Louisiana Territory gave the government what seemed like a way to end the struggle for land between white settlers and southeastern Native tribes—by resettling the tribes in the West. Between 1817 and 1837, the Choctaw, Muscogee (Creek), Chickasaw, Seminole, and Cherokee tribes all were persuaded or compelled to give up their ancestral homes in exchange for land and other allowances in the unknown territory beyond the fringe of settlement—a huge swath of timber and prairie north of the Red River, overlapping the Osage and Plains Indians' buffalo-hunting grounds. Many tribal leaders accepted the move to the new "Indian Territory" as inevitable, but the Seminole and most of the Cherokee resisted removal and were forcibly evicted by the army. The move

The Trail of Tears by Robert Lindneux, 1942. In the winter of 1838, the politics of "Indian Removal" forced a Cherokee exodus: 15,000 tribal members traveled 900 miles across 8 states to Indian Territory. *Woolaroc Museum*

west was grueling for all five tribes but particularly bitter for the Cherokee, who traveled as prisoners of war: a third of the tribe died in a series of journeys that became known as the Trail of Tears.

Once in Indian Territory, the tribes made their rich new land home. The Choctaw established schools, churches, and cotton plantations along the Red River, while the Cherokee founded their capital on the green banks of the Illinois River. There they published the state's first newspaper and built the first men's and women's seminaries west of the Mississippi River. ♦

Above: Sequoyah, a Cherokee born in Tuskeegee, Tennessee, spent 12 years analyzing his language, identifying 86 sounds for which he invented written symbols. His alphabet, shown in this 1836 lithograph, enabled the Cherokee to become largely literate within a generation. *The Granger Collection. Right:* Choctaws of two races, c. 1900. Escaped African slaves were welcomed by the Southeast tribes. *William Loren Katz Collection*

"When I was a boy, the country where we lived was full of wild game, deer, turkeys, and there were bears on the mountains and plenty of fish in the Kiamichi River. We lived on the river and we could see the fish floating on top of the water… We used our bows and arrows for fishing….We killed deer any time we wanted and turkey, too."

Gilbert Thompson, describing the pre–Civil War Choctaw Nation to a WPA worker in the 1930s

Creek Women Cooking Fish by Acee Blue Eagle, c. 1950. Blue Eagle, of Creek-Pawnee descent, was among the first commercially successful American Indian artists. He founded the influential Native American art school at Bacone College in Muskogee. *Philbrook Museum of Art, Tulsa*

Fort Gibson by Vinson Lackey, c. 1950s. Fort Gibson, on the Arkansas frontier, was one of several forts built in the 1820s to guard the border with Indian lands. Lackey shows the fort as it was in the 1840s. *Gilcrease Museum, Tulsa*

At the outbreak of the Civil War, both the Arkansas Territory and Texas joined the Confederacy, and U.S. soldiers were pulled out of Indian Territory forts that were supposed to protect the Five Tribes from incursions by the Osage and Plains tribes. Feeling abandoned, Choctaw and Chickasaw leaders soon signed an alliance with the Confederates. The Cherokee and Muscogee (Creek) were so divided on the issue of secession that the war effectively ignited civil strife within both tribes. The most significant battle in Indian Territory was fought at a pasture near Honey Springs, a Confederate supply depot. Union troops prevailed, but the battle is best remembered as the first time in American history that whites, Native Americans, and blacks fought alongside one another.

The Five Tribes paid a price for siding with the Confederacy: new treaties signed after the Civil War took land away for the resettlement of Indians from other parts of the West and granted rights of way for railroads. Over the next two decades, dozens of tribes and tribal remnants, with varying languages and customs, came to live on reservations in Indian Territory. Forts were built to limit the hunting grounds of the nomadic Comanches, Kiowas, Cheyenne, and Arapaho. The railroads helped buffalo hunters work with deadly efficiency, enraging and impoverishing the Plains tribes who had followed and depended on the creature for centuries. ▲

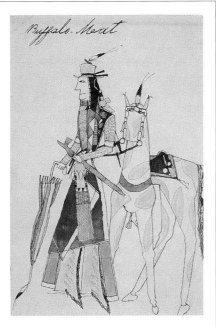

Above: Self-Portrait by Buffalo Meat (Cheyenne), 1878. Buffalo Meat was one of the best-known of these "ledger drawing" artists imprisoned after an 1874 rebellion. *Oklahoma Historical Society. Left:* Civil War banner of the Cherokee Braves. *General Sweeney's Museum, Republic, Missouri*

> *"Creation! Hell! That took six days.*
> *This was done in one!"*
>
> Edna Ferber, Cimarron, *1930*

Panel from the mural *Land Run* by Charles Banks Wilson, in the Oklahoma State Capitol, dedicated 1976. *Photo Tim Thompson*

At high noon on April 22, 1889, a pistol crack and cannon fire announced Oklahoma's future with the start of the 1889 Land Run, a tumultuous dash for homesteads and town sites on 2 million acres in the heart of the territory. Would-be homesteaders had agitated over nearly a decade for access to land ceded to the government by

Left: The line outside of the Guthrie land office on the opening day. *San Francisco Public Library*
Below: In 1926, Ponca City oilman E. W. Marland invited nationally prominent sculptors to create an archetypal "Pioneer Woman." Bryant Baker's winning design, cast in bronze, stands 17 feet high. *Photo Tim Thompson*

Indian tribes; the run was dubbed "Harrison's Hoss Race" for President William Henry Harrison, who signed the proclamation granting their wish. Men and women came from all corners of the globe for what was billed as a last hurrah for free land—galloping in on Kentucky thoroughbreds and Texas cow ponies, arriving on foot, by mule-drawn wagon, or on special trains commanded to travel no faster than a man on horseback. By nightfall of the first day, 50,000 settlers had staked claims; 10,000 alone pitched tents on a bend in the Canadian River, the future site of Oklahoma City. Over the next five years, the federal government allotted homesteads to Native tribes in western Oklahoma, and opened the remaining land to settlement in five more land runs—each more chaotic than the last. ▲

Longhorns Watering on a Cattle Drive by Ila McAfee, 1941. This is one of several Oklahoma murals McAfee painted. *Gilcrease Museum, Tulsa*

Indian Territory's Native American residents had used the land lightly, leaving it to others to exploit the state's abundant reserves of coal, oil, timber, and rich grass. Cattle became the state's first major industry; after the Civil War, the prairies where buffalo once grazed were put into service to fatten herds of longhorn cattle, which moved north from Texas along a network of trails through Indian Territory. ♠

When Cattle Was King

Three major cattle trails ran through Indian Territory after the Civil War: the Chisholm Trail, Western Trail, and Old Shawnee Trail. The most famous of them, named for Cherokee trader Jesse Chisholm, became the conduit for some 5 to 7 million head of cattle between 1867 and 1884. The Chisholm Trail led from the Red River directly into the luxuriant grass of the Cherokee Outlet in north-central Oklahoma. By the 1880s, the cattle industry had put down roots in the Outlet and Osage prairies, as sprawling ranches—complete with their own rail lines and shipping stations—were established.

A gate at Windward Stud Ranch in Norman. Cattle drovers may have hated fences, but ranchers love their gates. Many an entrance to an Oklahoma spread boasts ornate ironwork, most often worked with a Western theme or featuring the ranch cattle brand. *Photo David Stocklein*

"TO ALL THOSE WHO SAW THAT LONG LINE OF TEXAS cattle come up over a rise in the prairie, nostrils wide for the smell of water, dust-caked and gaunt, so ready to break from the nervous control of the riders strung out along the flanks of the herd, there came the feeling that in this spectacle there was something elemental, something resistless, something perfectly in keeping with the unconquered land about them."

Ernest Staples Osgood, The Day of the Cattleman, *1929*

"Surpassing All Truthfulness"

Advertisement for Pawnee Bill's Wild West Show

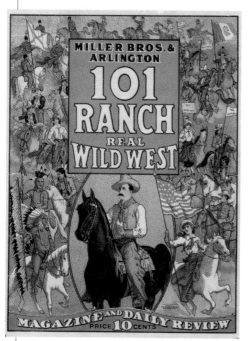

Part circus, part roundup, and only sporadically real, the Wild West shows that toured between the 1880s and World War I gave American and European audiences their first glimpse of the cowboy as hero. Two notable shows sprang from the Cherokee Outlet's buffalo prairies. In 1888, Gordon "Pawnee Bill" Lillie, a sometime partner of Buffalo Bill Cody, organized Pawnee Bill's Historical Wild West Exhibition and Indian Encampment, which toured the U.S. and Europe with a lineup that included Mexican *vaqueros,* Pawnee Indians, staged attacks on a wagon train, white buffaloes, dancing elephants, and Lillie's sharpshooter wife, May. The Miller Brothers' 101 Ranch Show, a sideline of the storied 101 Ranch, was better known and studded with stars: Will Rogers perfected his roping act there, performing with movie cowboy Tom Mix and Bill Pickett, the African-American inventor of bulldogging. Geronimo himself was brought up from Fort Sill for the show's inaugural performance, which climaxed in a buffalo hunt and feast. ♠

Opposite: Cover of *101 Ranch Real Wild West Magazine and Daily Review,* c. 1911. *Western History Collections, University of Oklahoma Library*
Below: Poster for Pawnee Bill's Historic Wild West, 1894. *The Granger Collection, New York*

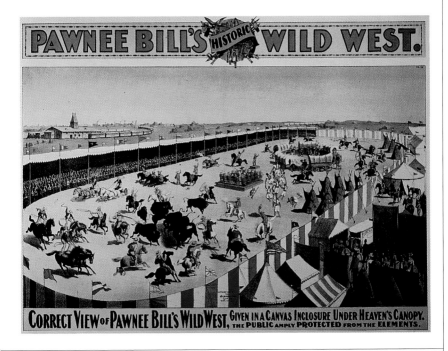

Right: Shamrock by James Gordley, c. 1975. Gordley's folk paintings depicted many of Oklahoma's oil boomtowns during the early 1900s. In 1915, during the Creek County boom, Shamrock exploded from 35 to 10,000 residents (today's residents number 95). All its streets were given Irish names and all buildings were painted green. Private collection. Photo courtesy Oklahoma Today. Below: Panorama of Burbank, Oklahoma, 1922. *Photo Phillips Petroleum Company. Opposite:* Sticker for the International Petroleum Exposition, held in Tulsa in 1938. *Private collection*

In the 1820s, the Cherokees noticed oil shimmering on springs in Indian Territory and skimmed the residue from the water's surface with feathers to use as a cure for rheumatism. Oklahoma's commercial oil industry didn't begin until 1897, when the Nellie Johnstone Num-

ber One, near Bartlesville, erupted with a towering spume. "Black gold" created fabulous fortunes and scores of boisterous, wide-open boomtowns as a number of huge underground pools were discovered in the next decades—first in northeastern Oklahoma, later in the central and south-central regions. Oklahoma entered the Union in 1907 as the largest oil-producing state, a rank it held until 1928. ♠

"IT TAKES LUCK TO FIND OIL...BEST OF ALL ARE LUCK and skill in proper proportion, but don't ask what the proportion should be. In case of doubt, weigh mine with luck."

Oilman and collector Everette L. DeGolyer

Oil Talk

Cherry picker
An implement for retrieving tools dropped in a drilling hole

Darb
From boomtown entertainer Ruby Darby; something exceptional was termed "a real darb."

Dead-in-a-hurry
A worker who hauled nitroglycerine

Jackknife
A portable derrick

Pebble puppy
A newly degreed geologist

Roughneck
A rotary-drilling rig worker

Roustabout
An oil lease worker

Tool pusher
Foreman of a drilling crew

Wildcat
A well drilled on unproved land

Legacies of Oil

Oklahoma's oil barons spent prodigious amounts of money on themselves, yet had ample cash left over to create a legacy of art and architecture that endures today. The Philbrook Museum of Art and the Gilcrease Museum in Tulsa, and the Woolaroc Museum near Bartlesville were all founded and endowed by oil magnates. Oil built the state's signature skylines: Tulsa's glory days as the "Oil Capital of the World" coincided with Art Deco's heyday, and the city's collection of Art Deco buildings is surpassed only by Miami and New York City. Oil continues to be one of Oklahoma's top industries—between 1890 and 1990, the state's 400,000 oil and gas wells produced 13.5 billion barrels of oil and 67 trillion cubic feet of natural gas.

The Reign of Cotton

Snowy fields of cotton once covered thousands of acres in Indian Territory, much of it planted in the fertile Red River valley by mixed-blood Choctaw plantation owners. Most prominent of these was Robert M. Jones, who owned a trading company in Kentucky before moving west on the Choctaw Trail of Tears in 1831. At its height, Jones's fortune included 28 trading stores, six cotton plantations, a Louisiana sugar plantation, two steamboats, and a white-pillared mansion called Rose Hill. The Choctaw, like the other Five Civilized Tribes, had brought slaves with them to Indian Territory, and Jones became one of Indian Territory's largest slaveholders—and the Territory's leading secessionist during the Civil War.

By the 1920s, a quarter of Oklahoma's farms grew cotton, and a thousand gins operated in the state. A decade later, drought and economic depression caused a dramatic, permanent decline in cotton production.

Vintage postcard of families picking cotton in Oklahoma, c. 1920s. Cotton's most enduring legacy in Oklahoma is a spiritual, popularized by a minister at a Choctaw boarding school who overheard former slaves Wallis and Minerva Willis singing "Swing Low, Sweet Chariot." *Private collection*

Tulsa's Boston Avenue Methodist Church is a striking example of modern ecclesiastical architecture. Its design was conceived by Tulsa artist Adah Robinson and executed by Tulsa architects Rush, Endicott, and Goff. Construction was completed in 1929. *Photo Michael Hardeman*

Oklahoma is sometimes called "the Buckle of the Bible Belt," an appellation it earns with an awe-inspiring number and variety of churches. Indian Territory was peppered with Catholic, Presbyterian, Methodist, and Quaker missions, and homesteaders immediately set about organizing churches, holding services the first Sunday after the 1889 Land Run. Mainstream Protestantism attracted the most members, but onion-shaped Russian Orthodox domes rose over the prairie, along with the plain wooden buildings favored by Mennonite and Amish farmers.

The Cheyenne and Kiowa practiced the Sun Dance on the southern plains, and in the 1880s many flocked to

the Ghost Dance, a messianic movement that promised to restore the old ways—and the buffalo. John Wilson, a Caddo, and Comanche chief Quanah Parker helped spread different versions of a peyote rite, formally incorporated in Oklahoma as the Native American Church in 1918. ♠

Left: Members of the Delaware, an eastern woodlands tribe, brought their woodcarving traditions when they were relocated to Oklahoma a century ago. On the left, *bois d'arc* shaman's staff; right, a cedar longhouse prayer staff, both by Delaware carver James Watkins. Spiritual traditions inform the making and use of these staffs. *Southern Plains Indian Museum and Crafts Center, Anadarko. Below:* Quanah Parker on horseback. *University of Oklahoma Library*

"THE FIRST RELIGIOUS SERVICE TO BE HELD in the new town of Watonga was on Sunday following the opening…held by a preacher who had been a missionary in Siam, who was home on a vacation and had drifted to the new territory. It was a queer crowd of folk who attended, but an orderly one, no shots fired and no one killed."

Mrs. Tom B. Ferguson, They Carried the Torch: The Story of Oklahoma's Pioneer Newspapers, *1937. Mrs. Ferguson was Edna Ferber's model for Sabra in* Cimarron.

Illustration by Mike Wimmer from the picture book *Train Song*. Even as railroads helped build Oklahoma towns, they erased others. After Reno City residents miscalculated by a few miles the path the Rock Island line would take, they moved the whole town 10 miles south and rechristened it El Reno. *Courtesy the artist*

Iron Horse, Iron Road

Choctaw Indians called the rail lines built through the Winding Stair Mountains to haul out carloads of timber and coal the "iron road." In central and western Oklahoma, the railroads preceded the homesteaders; railroad interests were among those lobbying the hardest for settlement of Indian Territory. When settlers poured in, entire stores with prefabricated walls were shipped to the territory by rail, enabling store owners to open up shop in a matter of days. During the first hard years, as settlers struggled to "prove up" their claims, railroads protected their markets by bringing the farmers wheat seed at cost.

Homeland of Route 66

Not yet a state when cars first appeared on American roads, Oklahoma grew up with the automobile. And in 1926, Tulsa highway engineer Cyrus Avery put the state on the map when he convinced federal officials to piece together a new transcontinental highway—Route 66—from remnants of the old Ozark Trail in his home state. "After 66 came, we knew where we were and we knew we could go somewhere," said a Muskogee businessman. Dust Bowl refugees poured out of the state along the Mother Road in the 1930s, and throngs of tourists poured in after World War II, rolling through hilly northeastern Oklahoma right to the doorstep of the West. Oklahoma's trading posts, selling beaded moccasins and handmade trinkets, helped define a souvenir genre, while alligator and buffalo ranches, tourist courts, and neon-lit diners beckoned to weary travelers.

Will Rogers Motor Court neon sign on Oklahoma's Route 66. More than 400 miles of Route 66 can still be driven in the state, and in eastern Oklahoma's small towns, clattering coffee shops, roadside parks, and a slow, sweet pace preserve the spirit of the road along with its outlines. *Photo Terrence Moore*

"HIGHWAY 66 IS THE MAIN MIGRANT road. 66—the long concrete path across the country, waving gently up and down on the map, from the Mississippi to Bakersfield— over the red lands and the gray lands, twisting up into the mountains, crossing the Divide and down into the bright and terrible desert, and across…to the mountains again, and into the rich California valleys."

John Steinbeck, The Grapes of Wrath, *1939*

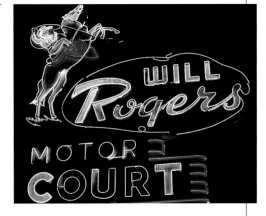

Below: The Mountain Fork River at Beavers Bend State Park. *Opposite above:* Treasure Lake in the Wichita Mountains. *Both photos, Michael Hardeman. Opposite below:* Tucker Tower, near Ardmore, rises 100 feet above Lake Murray. Reportedly intended for use as retreat for Oklahoma governors, it's now home to a geological museum and nature center. *Photo Kent and Donna Dannen*

"LAKE TEXOMA WAS BORN OF SUFFERING. THE RED RIVER IN seven raging floods beginning in 1843 all but drowned the… bottom-lands. Nearly thirteen million acre-feet of flood-waters swept down the Red River in the angry flood of 1908."

Robert S. Kerr, Land, Wood and Water, *1960*

An ironic corollary to the dusty heartbreak of the 1930 was the perennial watery plague farmers suffered as Oklahoma's rivers raged out of their banks after spring and autumn rains. The wild rivers have since been tamed by numerous dams, giving Oklahoma—a state without a single natural lake—more miles of shoreline than the Atlantic and Gulf coasts combined. Lake Texoma, created from the Red and Blue Rivers on the state's southern border, spreads into three counties; the mile-long Pensacola Dam, which spans the Grand Lake O' the Cherokees in the northeast, is the longest multiple-arch dam in the world. Along with flood control, the manmade lakes provided new play-

grounds. In seven state parks, Works Progress Administration craftsmen quarried sandstone and felled trees, using the native materials to fashion stone-lined paths and artful cabins, picnic shelters, and bathhouses. One park, Quartz Mountain State Park, today is home to the Oklahoma Arts Institute, a regional center for music, writing, dance, and visual arts education. ♠

Murals and Monuments

The walls of downtown Hominy, a tiny town in northeastern Oklahoma, are adorned with 40 murals on Native American and Western themes. This one, by local artist Cha' Tullis, was painted in the 1990s.
Photo David G. Fitzgerald

Oklahoma's wide-open spaces and larger-than-life history make it eminently well suited to portrayal in murals, which adorn the walls of Oklahoma post offices, state office buildings, even the statehouse ceilings. The buffalo-hide tipis painted by the Kiowa and Comanche invited a natural segue into a series of symbol-rich murals painted for federal and state buildings; many of their creators attended a mural school established at the Fort Sill Indian school in the 1930s. Monumental sculpture is at home on the plains, too. The

clean, emotional lines chiseled by the masterful Chiricahua Apache sculptor Allan Houser can be seen around the state, near the front steps of the state capitol, and along a lonely two-lane highway that leads to the Apache headquarters near Lawton. Visitors to Tulsa will find a wealth of public art, ranging from bronze figures to abstract installations—thanks in part to an ordinance requiring a small percentage of all public building funds to be spent on art.

Above: Holding the Claim by Harold Holden, 1993. Holden's sculpture in Enid commemorates the 1893 Cherokee Strip land run. *Photo John Elk III. Left: Sacred Rain Arrow* by Allan Houser, 1988. This bronze stands in front of the Gilcrease Museum in Tulsa. The grandson of Geronimo, Houser (1914–80) showed early artistic talent, and by the 1930s his paintings were sought after. He began sculpting in 1948, transferring the themes and style of his painting to three dimensions. Houser's sculptures have been displayed from Oklahoma's state capitol to the White House. *Photo Gail Mooney*

In the 1890s, Guthrie was the capital and queen city of Oklahoma Territory, its red-brick streets lined with turreted mansions and grand commercial buildings—many of them the work of architect Joseph Foucart, said to have been lured away from Belgian royalty. In 1910, politics and a statewide referendum shifted the capital to Oklahoma City, in a move still described by some as larceny. Guthrie went into shock for seven decades, not prosperous enough to seriously revamp its blocks of Victorian buildings as styles changed. In the 1980s, armed with federal grants and elbow grease, Guthrie resurrected a living museum hidden beneath layers of aluminum siding. Townspeople uncovered expanses of stained-glass windows and pressed tin ceilings, spiffed up miles of carved moldings and intricate brickwork, and even found a few gas lamps flickering around town. A full 400 blocks of Victorian residential and Prairie commercial architecture have been placed on the National Register of Historic Places, making Guthrie the largest urban district of its kind anywhere. ▲

Above: Painted sign on a restored building on Guthrie's Harrison Avenue advertises Coca-Cola at a 1920s price. The buildings along First Street and Harrison Avenue are a land run legacy. *Photo John Elk III. Left:* Victorian facades in downtown Guthrie. *Photo David G. Fitzgerald Opposite:* The main auditorium in Guthrie's grand Scottish Rite Temple. Built in the 1920s the marble and stone edifice reflects historical periods including imperial Rome, ancient Egypt, Georgian England, and Gothic France. *Photo Tim Thompson*

YEARS OF DUST

RESETTLEMENT ADMINISTRATION
Rescues Victims
Restores Land to Proper Use

Above: Years of Dust, WPA-era poster by Ben Shahn, 1936. © VAGA, New York/ The Granger Collection
Right: Campaign button. University of Oklahoma
Opposite: Governor "Alfalfa Bill" Murray in all-night session, 1932. Corbis-Bettmann

It is completely in character with Oklahoma's commonsense politics that its capitol in Oklahoma City—a granite and limestone Greco-Roman edifice built in 1914–17 on a former cow pasture—conspicuously lacks a dome. Architect Solomon Layton designed one on an alternate blueprint, but a wartime steel shortage blocked any talk of dome-building; then in the 1920s, legislators decided it would be a frivolous expense. "[A dome] is not anymore an evidence of sovereignty than a dress suit is an indication of a gentleman," one declared.

Oklahoma politicians have long wooed voters by appealing to their practicality and by cultivating the folksy image perfected by humorist and political sage Will Rogers, an Oologah native. Former governor Robert S. Kerr, one of Oklahoma's most beloved statesmen, conceded to wearing a business suit in Washington but changed into work pants and red suspenders before get-

In a state rich with colorful politicians, William "Alfalfa Bill" Murray was the most eccentric—an embarrassment or an inspiration, depending on where you stood. Born in Texas, Murray, a lawyer, married into the Chickasaw tribe and in 1905 helped organize the Sequoyah Convention, an unsuccessful attempt to create an all-Indian state, and in 1906 presided over Oklahoma's Constitutional Convention. After losing a bid for governor in 1910, Murray—a champion of agriculture and an enthusiastic promoter of alfalfa—started a (doomed) agricultural colony in Bolivia. Returning to the state, he was elected governor in 1932. In office, he wielded power flamboyantly, calling out the National Guard a record 34 times. Utterly immune to public opinion, Murray sent a telegram telling the entire U.S. Supreme Court to go to hell, and he planted vegetables and grazed cattle on the front lawn of the governor's mansion.

ting off the train back home. There was substance beneath the style: Oklahoma, the fourth youngest state, was born during the national Progressive movement and has a strongly populist tradition. Its constitution—packed with provisions for direct democracy, employee and consumer protection, and corporate regulations—was hailed as the most radical of all the state constitutions when crafted in 1907. It was by far the longest: at ratification, it took three days to read out loud. ♠

Right: An Oklahoma sod house, c. 1890s. *Western History Collections, University of Oklahoma Libraries*

Below: Oilman and governor E. W. Marland modeled his 52-room Italian Renaissance–style villa in Ponca City after the Davanzati Palace in Florence, finishing its interior with Waterford chandeliers from Ireland, a wooden throne from Germany, and gold-leaf ceilings painted by imported Italian craftsmen. It's now a luxury inn. *Photo Tim Thompson*

Homes on the Range

Building materials varied greatly in early Oklahoma. Native Americans and settlers built log cabins in the east, but residents on the treeless western plains had to find other

resources. The Wichita covered the dome-shaped frames of their houses with grass thatch, while the Kiowa and Comanche lived in portable buffalo-hide tipis. (Coronado called them "little field tents.") Western settlers cut blocks of dense sod from the prairies and laid them like bricks.

In this century, Oklahoma's royalty, the oil barons, have tended to model their homes after castles, importing European craftsmen for

months at a time. In Ponca City, E. W. Marland's Italian Renaissance mansion was surrounded by gardens inspired by English and French models, ringed by moat-like pools. Oklahomans of more moderate means embraced the Arts and Crafts movement's emphasis on natural materials, and the state's temperate climate is congenial to the wide porches, open floor plans, and abundant windows typical of the Prairie school of architecture. Architect Bruce Goff, who directed the University of Oklahoma School of Architecture in the 1940s and 50s, worked in an organic style pioneered by Frank Lloyd Wright. Goff's innovative use of such materials as surplus nose cones from World War II airplanes, coal, broken glass, goose feathers, and glass ashtrays harkened back to the state's first imaginative and pragmatic builders.

This home in Bartlesville, known as Shin'en Kan, was designed in 1955 by Bruce Goff for Joe Price of the oil pipeline family. It took 23 years to build and was destroyed in a fire in 1996. Goff, an heir to the organic tradition pioneered by Frank Lloyd Wright, was hailed by one critic for raising "making do" to an art form. *Photo David G. Fitzgerald*

"Well, I've been to Buckingham Palace, but it hasn't anything on Waite Phillips's house."

Will Rogers

Tulsa oilman Waite Phillips built Villa Philbrook—now the Philbrook Museum of Art—in the style of a Florentine villa. The gardens that surround it contain many of the design elements favored by European aristocracy—reflecting pools, a walled garden, a French "temple of love"—plus a few Oklahoma adaptations. Landscape designer Herbert Hare substituted Russian olive trees for true olives, and eastern red cedars stood in for Italian cypress—including one specimen of red cedar aptly named for its setting: "Derrick." The formal gardens are planted with bands of American desert yuccas, forming a lively contrast to formal hedges and a transition to the relaxed aesthetic of the natural landscape that covers 20 acres of the estate. The design for the garden was often altered because Phillips hated to cut down trees. And he never forgot the roots of his fortune: some nights, he directed the formal gardens to be lit with leftover oilfield flares. ♠

Opposite and above: Villa Philbrook in Tulsa is set in 23 acres of gardens. The former home of Waite Phillips, now the Philbrook Museum of Art, it contains world-class collections of Native American and European art. *Photos, Howard Robson and Tim Thompson. Left:* Woolaroc Lodge near Bartlesville was Frank Phillips's hunting lodge, built of logs and filled with rustic furniture, Native American textiles, and elkhorn chandeliers. It too is now a museum, housing Western art and artifacts. *Woolaroc Museum*

Right: The Oklahoma Room in the Governor's Mansion. First Lady Cathy Keating commissioned a carpet with the state seal for the room. *Below:* This elaborately carved mahogany bed (c. 1850) once belonged to Emperor Maximilian of Mexico. Thought to have arrived in Oklahoma around the time of the land runs, it is among many antiques from both museums and private collections in the mansion. *All photos courtesy Office of the First Lady of Oklahoma*

Oklahoma's Dutch Colonial–style governor's residence was a showplace when it was built in 1928, but after nearly seven decades of use, it had become a shadow of its former self. In 1995, First Lady Cathy Keating organized the stately equivalent of a barn raising, pulling together a team of seven interior designers from around the state, and an army of donors. Private funds paid for the restoration of historical details including windows, paneling, and moldings, and individual donors filled formerly threadbare rooms with family

heirlooms. Oklahoma museums chipped in artwork on loan, the Oklahoma Historical Society loaned an ornately carved Renaissance Revival bed imported during the land runs, and carpets were commissioned, to be emblazoned with the state seal and the names of Oklahoma Native America tribes. During a housewarming held to celebrate the basement-to-attic restoration, Oklahomans brought in the finishing touches, including china, crystal, and silver—and a place mat purchased by an elementary school class. ♠

The Governor's Mansion was designed and built by the Oklahoma City firm of Layton, Hicks and Forsyth. Oklahoma citizens donated more than 1,500 items to the restoration. Hidden from view in the backyard is an Oklahoma-shaped swimming pool; the panhandle is a hot tub.

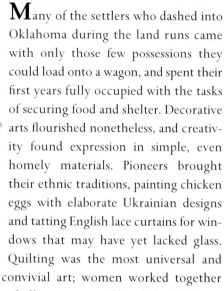

Many of the settlers who dashed into Oklahoma during the land runs came with only those few possessions they could load onto a wagon, and spent their first years fully occupied with the tasks of securing food and shelter. Decorative arts flourished nonetheless, and creativity found expression in simple, even homely materials. Pioneers brought their ethnic traditions, painting chicken eggs with elaborate Ukrainian designs and tatting English lace curtains for windows that may have yet lacked glass. Quilting was the most universal and convivial art; women worked together piecing scraps of silk or squares of hand-dyed tobacco sacks and vied with each other at county fairs to see who had made the tiniest, most even stitches. Quilt-

Above: Oklahoma City artist Kathy Kise Smith painted, tiled, and embellished this chest, salvaged from a pasture after a tornado. Smith named her creation "Dorothy." *Photo David G. Fitzgerald*
Right: Kickapoo/Sac and Fox bead artist Judy Coser worked traditional designs into these Northern Sac and Fox moccasins. Coser, a member of the Potato Clan, lives in Mounds. *Photo David Crenshaw*

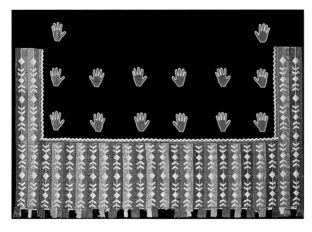

Left: Osage blanket/shawl, c. 1915. Osage needle-workers, past and present, are renowned for their embroidered and finger-woven textiles. The designs usually express the tribal concept of duality, centered on the division of earth and sky. *America Hurrah Archive, New York. Below:* Coiled pot by Anna Mitchell (Cherokee). Working with clay found on her own land, near Vinta, led Mitchell to research and re-create the coil technique and styles of traditional Cherokee pottery. *Photo David Crenshaw*

ing extended into Oklahoma's Native American homes as well; the Seminole were known for using cloth in brilliant colors. Artful objects inhabited the everyday life of Oklahoma tribes: finely wrought Cherokee baskets and clay water jugs, stunning beaded cradleboards for Kiowa and Comanche children, and the beautifully painted rawhide bags—*parfleche*—used by the Cheyenne to carry dried meat. ▲

"MY HUSBAND HAD ALWAYS WANTED A PIPE LIKE Sequoyah's—a little clay pipe with a reed stem—because he was descended from him. So…that was the beginning. I didn't know anything about working with clay. It was all from trial and error."

Anna Mitchell, named a Cherokee National Living Treasure, 1998

Beef has been the mainstay of Oklahoma tables since the cattle drover days. By proclamation, Oklahoma's official meal is the delicacy known as chicken-fried steak—a generous piece of beef battered, fried, and served with cream gravy. Another state obsession is barbecue, where an unwritten law applies: the meat is flavorful in inverse proportion to the slickness of the establishment in which it is consumed. (Heaven itself is when barbecue is served on squares of butcher paper.) It's hard to go hungry in Oklahoma, where cooks combine the Midwestern love of garden produce with Southern indulgence. A typical blue-plate special might come piled with both flaky biscuits and rich cornbread, fried chicken, brown beans, green beans cooked with onion, sliced garden tomatoes, pickled cucumbers, and fresh corn, topped off with pie— coconut cream with mile-high meringue is a Route 66 classic. ♠

Above: Basket of okra. *Photo Michelle Garrett/Corbis. Right:* Diners from 34 countries have found their way to Phil's Country Fare in Westville, population 1,374, for Phil's legendary thick steaks. "I don't cut anything less than an inch thick," he says.

Photo David Crenshaw. Opposite: Cardboard cut-out from Gene Autry's Melody Ranch Cut-Out Dolls, 1950. Real chuck wagons weren't generally as shipshape as this depiction of Autry's outfit. *Courtesy John Gilman and Robert Heide*

Fruits of the Fields

Thanks to geography, Oklahoma's soil yields distinct regional specialties. The Ozark Plateau, in the northeast, is strawberry and huckleberry country. Peaches abound in central Oklahoma, and thickets of wild sand plums are harvested in the west. Cowboys reported shaking the bounty out of pecan trees as they traveled through Indian Territory; in the 1830s it was a crime to cut down a pecan tree in the Choctaw Nation. Okra, a vegetable that loves summer heat, has its own festival in Checotah, and sorghum molasses is celebrated in Wewoka, where batches are cooked up over a wood fire at the annual Sorghum Festival.

Hayhauler's Pie

4 cups fresh peaches,
    peeled and sliced
½ cup butter, softened
1½ cups sugar
1 cup flour
1 tsp. baking powder
½ tsp. salt
½ milk
½ tsp. vanilla
1 tsp. cornstarch
1 cup boiling water

Heat oven to 375° F and place peaches in a lightly greased 12 x 8 x 2-inch pan. Set aside. Cream butter and ¾ cup of the sugar, beating well. Combine flour, baking powder, and salt; add to creamed mixture, mixing well. Stir in milk and vanilla. Pour batter over peaches. Combine remaining ¾ cup sugar and cornstarch; stir in boiling water. Pour mixture over batter and bake 45 to 50 minutes.

GENE AUTRY
CHUCK WAGON

Cut on solid black line, fold back on dotted lines

George Shepherd was one of the throng of settlers to arrive at the spot that would become Oklahoma City during the 1889 Land Run. He would leave it to his daughters to stake a claim in the art world for the new state. Four of his six daughters painted; of those, Nellie Shepherd attained the most recognition, both for artistic achievement and for her founding of the Oklahoma City Art League—precursor of today's Oklahoma City Art Museum. Nellie left Oklahoma to study art in Cincinnati and in Paris, where her work was influenced by the Impressionists; in 1910 one of her paintings was selected for the prestigious Salon. Nellie died in 1920, while at work on a portrait of the Chickasaw storyteller Te Ata. In recent years, more attention has been paid to the work of the other Shepherd sisters, Nettie, Leona, and Myrtle; in fact, some early paintings attributed to Nellie may have been painted by Nettie. ♠

Above: Portrait of a Lady by Nettie Shepherd, c. 1900–10. Nettie accompanied Nellie to Italy in 1911 but died suddenly the same year. *Right: Trees* by Nellie Shepherd, c. 1913. *Both, Shepherd Manor Retirement Center.* None of the six sisters ever married, rare in their day, and several traveled abroad unchaperoned.

Te Ata by Nellie Shepherd, 1919–20. *Shepherd Manor Retirement Center*

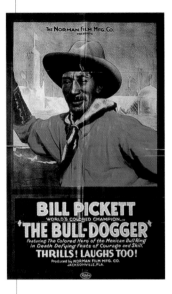

Above: Poster for a 1923 movie starring African-American cowboy Bill Pickett. *The Granger Collection, New York*
Right: These boots were custom-made for Jerry Croft in 1984 by Mike DeWitt, an instructor in the boot-making program at Oklahoma State University, Okmulgee. *Photo Mike DeWitt*

Ride 'em, Cowboy

Oklahomans work hard and play hard. Rodeo—a hard-working, competitive recreation if ever there was one—traces its Oklahoma roots back to 1882, when rancher Colonel George Miller organized an exhibition of roping and riding, featuring cowboys fresh from driving cattle up the Chisholm Trail. Two decades later, Miller's 101 Wild West Ranch Show gave the rodeo world a new event. After watching a cow dog immobilize a calf by biting it on the lip, 101 Ranch hand Bill Pickett tried it himself, and "bull-dogging" was born. Today, Oklahoma rodeos combine events designed purely for thrills—like bull riding—with top-notch displays of real ranching skills, like steer roping and bronc riding. (Bulldogging has given way to modern steer wrestling—no biting required.)

"IT IS A POOR COMMUNITY THAT cannot afford some anniversary for a pioneer celebration, with neighboring roundup clubs in the parade and a rodeo in the afternoon."

Angie Debo, Oklahoma Footloose and Fancy-Free, *1949*

Left: Rodeo bronc riding, Oklahoma City, 1970. *Photo William A. Allard/ National Geographic Society Image Collection* Oklahoma has more horses per capita than any other state. There are so many summer rodeos that August is known as "Cowboy Christmas." *Below:* OU's first football team, fielded in 1896, never made a touchdown or a first down. Things had improved by the time Bud Wilkinson (center) showed up in the late 1940s. *Western History Collections, University of Oklahoma Library*

Sooner Magic

Wresting a living from the plains called for strength, resolve, and occasional heroism—qualities that later made the sons of Oklahoma pioneers excel on the football field. But it was literature that launched the University of Oklahoma football juggernaut: OU regents, worried that John Steinbeck's Dust Bowl saga, *The Grapes of Wrath,* showed the state in a poor light, decided that a champion football team would convincingly highlight the state's vitality. For the next four decades, the OU Sooners did just that. Under coaches like Bud Wilkinson and Barry Switzer, they won six national titles and maintained the longest winning streak in the National Collegiate Athletic Association history—47 games.

The myriad Native American tribes gathered in what's now Oklahoma created a kaleidoscope of dances and rituals. Sacred tribal ceremonies, like the Muscogee (Creek) Green Corn dance and the Cheyenne Sun Dance, are still practiced privately, but in the late 19th century tribes began to come together for pan-Indian celebrations they called powwows. The Quapaw claim to have

held the first modern powwow more than a century ago, and today the

annual homecoming powwow is a summertime institution, open to all. Oklahoma powwows range from the Olympic-scale Red Earth—held each June in Oklahoma City and featuring competitive dances—to small family celebrations. The drum is said to carry the heartbeat of the people, and a drumming circle is the heart of any powwow. To untrained eyes the dancers' regalia is a gorgeous but confusing swirl of color and movement; in fact, each feather, color, and porcupine quill is imbued with significance. ♠

"*We Kiowa are old, but we dance.*

Our dance is spirited. Today's twisting path is temporary; the path will be gone tomorrow but the folk memory remains. Our forefathers' deeds touch us, shape us, like strokes of a painting. In endless procession, their deeds mark us."

James Auchiah (Kiowa),
in Kiowa voices, *volume 1, 1981*

One Sunday at Shawnee by Brenda Kennedy Grummer, 1979. *Philbrook Museum of Art* **Opposite above:** Members of the Creek-Eucha tribe take part in a Green Corn Dance each June. *Photo David Crenshaw* **Opposite below:** *Eagle Dancer* by Stephen Mopope, c. 1930. *National Cowboy Hall of Fame, Oklahoma City*

Stranger Than Fiction

Oklahoma writers have not needed to look far for colorful stories and characters—in fact, novelist Edna Ferber discarded some of her historical research for *Cimarron* because, she said, it was simply too fantastic to be believed. State archives have inspired great historians, including Daniel Boorstin and Angie Debo, who wrote groundbreaking works from her tiny hometown of Marshall. Great storytellers are born here, like

Above: This portrait of historian Angie Debo by Charles Banks Wilson hangs in the Oklahoma State Capitol. *Photo Fred Marvel. Right:* Ralph Ellison was born in Oklahoma City in 1914 and studied music at the Tuskegee Institute. In 1942, his great novel *The Invisible Man* won the National Book Award; its author was later awarded the Presidential Medal of Freedom. *Bernard Gotfryd/Archive Photos*

Tony Hillerman, creator of Southwestern mysteries; Jim Thompson, who penned the gritty crime thriller *The Grifters;* and newcomer Rilla Askew. Ralph Ellison based his masterpiece *The Invisible Man* on his experience growing up in Oklahoma City, and Tulsan S. E. Hinton was only 16 when she wrote the classic tale of teenage alienation, *The Outsiders.*

Ever since the Five Civilized Tribes negotiated with the government to have the state's first printing presses brought to Indian Territory, Native voices have strongly shaped the literary landscape. Among them are the 19th-century poet and journalist Alexander Posey, Kiowa novelist N. Scott Momaday, Osage writer John Joseph Mathews, and Osage poet Carter Revard.

"THE DIRT IS NOT THE FAMOUS RICH RED OF THE CIMARRON country, nor the blended sienna and verdigris and salmon of the haunted Deep Fork river bottoms in the central heart of Oklahoma, but a faded yellow brown, dun-colored, dusty in summer, clayey in spring, rock-ridden in all seasons."

Rilla Askew, The Mercy Seat, *1997*

"IT WAS THE CONTINENTAL REACH, BEYOND MAPS AND geography, beyond the accounts of the voyageurs, almost beyond the distance of dreams. It was the middle and immeasurable meadow of North America. It was the destination and destiny of ancients who…coming with dogs and travois, followed herds of huge, lumbering animals down the long, cold cordillera, following the visions of their shamans. It was the sun's range. Nowhere on earth was there a more perfect equation of freedom and space."

N. Scott Momaday, The Ancient Child, *1989*

Above: **Book jacket illustration by Robert Hunt from** *The Outsiders* **by S. E. Hinton.** *Courtesy the artist. Left: Preliminary Horse 3* **by N. Scott Momaday, 1994. Of his childhood, the poet, artist, and writer Momaday has written: "The house and arbor of the homestead on Rainy Mountain Creek in Oklahoma crackled and rang with Kiowa words, exclamations, and songs that even now I keep in my ear."** *LewAllen Contemporary Arts, Santa Fe*

> *"My ancestors didn't come on the Mayflower,*
> *but they met the boat."*
>
> Will Rogers

Will Rogers is easily Oklahoma's most beloved native son and was, in the words of Damon Runyon, "America's most accomplished human document. One-third humor. One-third humanitarian. One-third heart." Part Cherokee, Rogers was born in Indian Territory in 1879 and became an accomplished enough roper to be featured in the 101 Ranch Wild West Show. In 1916, when Rogers moved to New York to twirl a rope as a filler act at the Ziegfeld Follies, the wryly funny remarks he drawled onstage soon catapulted him into the spotlight. They also provided the basis for the Broadway show *Will Rogers Follies,* which won six Tony awards in 1991. A published collection of Rogers's Follies quotes led to a newspaper column, seasoned heavily with political observations and misspellings. In the 1920s, Rogers took his act to Hollywood, where he appeared in 71 movies; he was the top box-office draw in 1934. When Rogers died in an airplane crash with Oklahoma aviator Wiley Post in August 1935, he was the most popular man in America. He is buried at the Will Rogers Memorial in Claremore, beneath his most famous—and quintessentially Oklahoman—one-liner: "I never met a man I didn't like." ▲

"EVERYTHING IS FUNNY AS LONG AS IT is happening to somebody else."

The Illiterate Digest, *1924*

Left: Keith Carradine starred in the Broadway musical *Will Rogers Follies. Photo Martha Swope © Time, Inc. Above:* Statue of Will Rogers by Jo Davidson, 1938, at the Will Rogers Memorial Museum in Tulsa. *Photo Gail Mooney. Opposite:* The young Will Rogers, c. 1906, during his Wild West Show days. Rogers left home with his lariat to perform and travel all over the world, but he never forgot his Oklahoma roots. "Oklahoma is the heart, it's the vital organ of our national existence," he once declared. *Will Rogers Memorial Museum*

Right: Katharine Sergava and Marc Platt in the famous Agnes de Mille ballet sequence from the original stage production of *Oklahoma!*, 1943. *Photo Gjon Mili, Life Magazine © Time, Inc. Below:* Shirley Jones and Gordon MacRae in a scene from the film version. *Photofest.* An outdoor production of *Oklahoma!* is staged each summer evening from Memorial Day to Labor Day at the Discoveryland! theater near Sapulpa.

With an assist from Rodgers and Hammerstein, Oklahoma gave the world what is perhaps its best-loved musical. The long-running Broadway production and subsequent movie version of *Oklahoma!* were based on the play *Green Grow the Lilacs* by Claremore writer Lynn Riggs.

R&H and their collaborators replaced traditional folk songs chosen by Riggs with now-classic show tunes and groundbreaking dances, but the characters, a collection of earthy dreamers, are Riggs's own.

Oklahoma's own theater scene, far from drama centers in New York and California, has a history of embracing new work—Tulsa Theatre, for instance, was the first community theater to stage Thornton Wilder's *Our Town*. Ballet flourishes here, too, particularly in Tulsa. The critically acclaimed Tulsa Ballet Theatre was co-founded by Moscelyne Larkin, one of five remarkable Native American ballerinas from Oklahoma. Others include Yvonne Chouteau, Rosella Hightower, and Marjorie Tallchief, all of whose careers included dancing with the Ballets Russe de Monte Carlo. Maria Tallchief, Marjorie's sister, also danced in the Ballets Russes before moving east to join the New York City Ballet, where she married founder and choreographer George Balanchine. ♠

Action!

Movies set in Oklahoma don't need gratuitous car chases or explosions—there's plenty of natural drama.

Twister Special effects star in 1996 drama about tornado-chasers.

Eight Seconds Gritty 1990s biopic of bullrider Lane Frost, who died in action; Luke Perry starred

Red River 1940s classic with John Wayne and Montgomery Clift as cattle drovers on the Chisholm Trail, battling stampedes and Indians

Cimarron Lively film adaptation of the Edna Ferber land run novel

Oklahoma! Movie version of the musical starring Gordon MacRae and Shirley Jones

Maria Tallchief, 1952. Photograph by Milton H. Greene. Tallchief was born in Fairfax, the daughter of an Irish-Scottish mother and an Osage father. "As an American, I believe in great individualism," she once said. "That's the way I was brought up." *Milton H. Greene Archives*

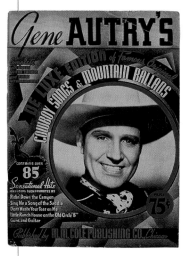

Way down yonder in the Indian Nation
A cowboy's life is my occupation
In the Oklahoma hills where I was born....

Woody Guthrie, "Oklahoma Hills"

Cowboy Crooners

"Western" music has enlivened the Oklahoma plains since cattle drovers calmed their charges with plaintive ballads about life on the range. Fiddles, mandolins, and guitars, easily transported on horseback, brought pioneer communities together for "play parties" or, religion permitting, dances—one early governor played the fiddle at Saturday night barn dances even while in office. Otto Gray and the Oklahoma Cowboys, a string band made up of ranch hands who toured the state in the 1920s, pioneered a genre popularized in the 1930s by Bob Wills and his Texas Playboys. The Playboys played Western swing: a blend of blues, old-time fiddle music, traditional folk, and ragtime that's been called

Above: A deluxe Gene Autry songbook published in 1936. Autry was discovered by Will Rogers in 1927 strumming a guitar at a Chelsea telegraph office. He later appeared in 93 movies. *Courtesy John Gilman and Robert Heide. Right:* Reba McEntire, a former barrel rider, was discovered when she sang "The Star Spangled Banner" at the National Finals Rodeo in Oklahoma City. *Courtesy MCA Records*

"Okie jazz"; they were heard for years in a daily live radio broadcast from Tulsa. One of the first singing cowboys to hit the silver screen was Gene Autry, who began a long line of country superstars from Oklahoma, including Conway Twitty, Garth Brooks, Reba McEntire, and Vince Gill.

Woody's Way

Folk poet Woody Guthrie was born in Okemah and came of age listening to country blues and ballads. Beset by family problems, Guthrie rolled west with his guitar during the Depression and lived the life of a troubadour, hymning the struggle of the weak against the powerful and the grace found in common places and people. Guthrie's music—and his insistence on being no one but himself—helped launch a folk songwriting tradition that endures today. Of the 1,000-plus songs Guthrie wrote in his lifetime, some were destined for greatness. His "Talkin' Dust Bowl Blues" raised spirits in his own time, and the anthem "This Land Is Your Land" has lifted hearts for generations.

"I HATE A SONG THAT MAKES YOU THINK YOU'RE NOT ANY GOOD. I hate a song that makes you think you are just born to lose. Bound to lose. No good to nobody. No good for nothing. Because you are either too old or too young or too fat or too slim or too ugly or too this or too that....Songs that run you down or songs that poke fun of you on account of your bad luck or your hard traveling. I am out to fight those kinds of songs to my very last breath of air and my last drop of blood."

Woody Guthrie, from a radio script, 1944

Woody Guthrie in the late 1930s. In 1998, Woody's hometown of Okemah unveiled a bronze bust of him and inaugurated an annual "Woody Guthrie Music Festival." (The music is free.) *Photo Frank Driggs/Corbis-Bettmann*

Right: The Blue Devils discovered "Little" Jimmy Rushing at work in his father's Oklahoma City lunchroom, singing and pouring root beer. *Photo Herb Snitzer/ StageImage. Below:* Chet Baker was born Chesney H. Baker in Yale, Oklahoma, in 1929; Baker's blues-tinged bebop trumpet style belied his roots—his father was a country-western guitarist. *Photo Herman Leonard/StageImage*

Oklahoma's reputation as a place where anyone with a will could make a life brought waves of black settlers near the turn of the century— some drawn by the Black State Movement's effort to create an African-American state. Blueswoman Bessie Smith later sang "Goin' to the Nation, Going to the Terr'tor'," echoing this urge for freedom and possibility. The movement fizzled, but the territory's black population swelled. In the next few next decades, it produced scores of accomplished musicians, including ragtime pianists and smoky blues players, but Oklahoma's largest imprint was on jazz. The Oklahoma City Blue Devils—called the best jazz band in the country in the 1920s—evolved from a brass marching band and in 1928 boasted an all-star lineup that included vocalist Little Jimmy Rushing, saxophonist Lester Young, and pianist William "Count" Basie. Guitarist Charlie Christian got his start playing barbecues around Oklahoma City; only 25 when he died in 1942, he was hailed as the world's best. Other innovators included bassist Oscar Pettiford, from Okmulgee—credited, along with Christian and Dizzy Gillespie, with developing bebop—and Muskogee native Claude "Fiddler" Williams, who pioneered jazz violin with Count Basie's orchestra. ♠

Count Basie. The nucleus of the legendary Count Basie Orchestra came together in the 1920s as the Oklahoma City Blue Devils. Along with Basie himself, other former Blue Devils were bassist Walter Page, saxophonist Lester Young, Jimmy Rushing, and Claude Williams. *Photo Herb Snitzer/Stagelmage*

"ON SUMMER EVENINGS, ANYONE MIGHT HALT THE CONVERSATION to exclaim 'Listen, they're raising hell down at Slaughter's Hall,' and we'd turn our heads westward to hear Jimmy's voice soar up the hill and down as pure and as miraculously unhindered by distance and earthbound things as is the body in youthful dreams of flying.

"'Now, that's the Right Reverend Jimmy Rushing preaching now, man,' someone would say."

Ralph Ellison on Little Jimmy Rushing, from Shadow and Act, *1964*

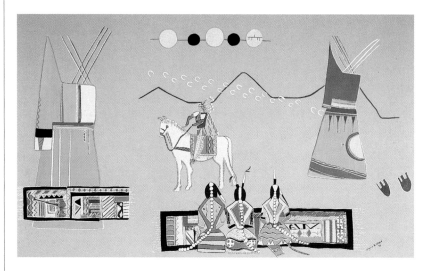

Return Home by Virginia Stroud, c. 1970. Stroud was only 17 years old when she won the Philbrook Museum of Art's Annual painting competition. Since then, she has made the ledger style her own. Of Cherokee/Creek descent, Stroud is an adopted Kiowa. *Philbrook Museum of Art, Tulsa*

Oklahoma's Native American artists have long been resourceful innovators. Captured chiefs of the southern Plains tribes, who traditionally painted on buffalo hide, began to work instead in ledger books supplied by prison guards. These early ledger drawings led directly to a flowering of Native painting in the 1930s and 40s—works rendered mostly in a flat style reminiscent of hide painting and rich with history and symbolism. The most famous painters of this era were the Kiowa Five, a group of Anadarko students whose talents were recognized by an Indian agent and nurtured at the University of

Oklahoma art department. Their success helped encourage a host of later artists who brought their tribal sensibilities to art, yet pushed genre boundaries. Their ranks include Blackbear Bosin, who painted traditional subjects with a dramatic flair; Cubist-inspired Benjamin Harjo, Jr.; modern ironist T. C. Cannon; and sculptor Allan Houser. Today, it seems there is no medium in which Oklahoma Native American artists aren't masters. ♠

Above: Collector No. 5 by T. C. Cannon (Kiowa–Caddo), 1975. Cannon broke new ground by combining Abstract Expressionism, Pop art, and Surrealism with Native American subjects. His brilliant career was cut short when he died in a car accident at the age of 31. *Private collection. Left: Shawnee Indians Having Cornbread Dance by* Earnest Spybuck, c. 1910. *National Museum of the American Indian*

Car Scaffold Burial (an outdoor sculpture/ installation) by Ron Anderson, 1984. Anderson, a Comanche, incorporates Plains burial tradition into this piece. *Collection the artist*

Far from major art centers, Oklahoma artists work in isolation—some would say splendid isolation—prompting them to look into their own experiences and emotions, not over their shoulders, for inspiration. Oklahoma's distinctive history also has had a hand in creating what one arts center director calls an "outlaw" heritage—a willingness to step outside of convention. In recent years, once-strict divisions between Western, Native American, and other styles of art have softened or disappeared. Native artists paint abstractions; those from other ethnic backgrounds confidently draw from their own heritage and histories. For many decades, Oklahoma artists were—with some exceptions—also isolated from Oklahoma art buyers, who went looking outside the state to build their collections. That situation, happily, has changed in the last few years, as galleries represent more local artists, and fewer artists leave the state in search of markets for their work. The growing strength of Oklahoma's artists is on display at the biennial exhibition of the Oklahoma Visual Artists Coalition and at a biennial "VisionMakers" exhibition, showcasing sculpture, fine arts, crafts, and other three-dimensional media. ♠

Above: Bob White at Night by Tom Palmore, 1998. Palmore underscores the mythic qualities of wild animals by painting them in fictional habitats. *Left: Flying Fruit* by Otto Duecker, 1997. *Both, J. Cacciola Galleries, New York*

Yes, in My Back Yard

Oil was discovered beneath Oklahoma City in 1928; in 1935, oilman-turned-governor E. W. Marland ordered wells drilled on the grounds of the state capitol and governor's mansion, despite city restrictions against them. (Marland called out the state militia to get the job done.) The wells are virtually dry now, including Petunia No. 1—named for the flower bed it displaced—but some of the derricks still stand.

Raising Cain's

In the 1930s and 40s, Bob Wills and the Texas Playboys turned Cain's Ballroom in Tulsa into a shrine to Western swing with their infectious live daily broadcasts on KVOO ("The Kind Voice of Oklahoma") and equally lively dances. The broadcasts and dances went on into the early 1960s. Such diverse acts as Gene Autry, Hank Williams, and the Sex Pistols have played the venerable old dance hall over the years.

Totem Pole Park

Shop teacher Ed Galloway spent more than two decades creating a fantasy roadside park in poured concrete on a little plot east of Foyil on State Highway 28A. The park's signature sculpture is a 60-foot totem pole embellished with Native American faces and bird, fish, and animal figures, painted in shades of pink, turquoise, and yellow. After Galloway's death, folk art enthusiasts banded together to restore and maintain the park.

A Whale of a Good Time

A beloved Route 66 roadside attraction, the Blue Whale is docked in a pond near Catoosa. The whale once lured travelers off the road with the promise of a cooling dip and a tour of a genuine "Alligator Ranch." (Both swimming in the pond and the alligators are things of the past.)

The Mother Road Enshrined

Clinton's Route 66 Museum is the first state museum to be dedicated to a highway— the fabled "Mother Road," which rolls right past the museum's front door. Inside, visitors take a decade-by-decade trip through the highway's history, from its construction in the 1920s by mule-drawn graders, to Dust Bowl refugees and 1950s neon-lit diners, right up to the 1970s, when the interstate system threatened to make the road obsolete. It couldn't be done, visitors will note. Route 66 is an American icon.

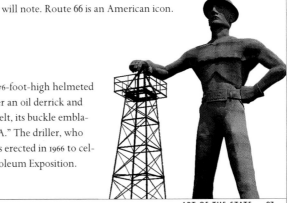

The Golden Driller

Tulsa's "Golden Driller" is a 76-foot-high helmeted oilfield worker, towering over an oil derrick and wearing a 48-foot-diameter belt, its buckle emblazoned with the word "TULSA." The driller, who wears a shoe size 393-DDD, was erected in 1966 to celebrate the International Petroleum Exposition.

Great People

Notable Oklahomans, mostly native-born, concentrating on the arts.

Garth Brooks (b. 1962), country music superstar

Gene Autry (1907–1998), cowboy actor and musician

Chet Baker (1929–1988), jazz trumpeter of the bebop era

John Berryman (1914–1972), Pulitzer Prize–winning poet

Daniel Boorstin (b. 1914), author and historian, former head of the Library of Congress

Charlie Christian (1916–1942), pioneering jazz guitarist

Angie Debo (1890–1988), "first lady of Oklahoma history"; wrote 13 books about frontier life

Ralph Ellison (1914–1994), African-American author of *The Invisible Man*, also a musician

Chester Gould (1900–1985), creator of "Dick Tracy"

Tony Hillerman (b. 1925), writer of mysteries set in Navajoland

Allan Houser (1914–1994), Chiricahua Apache painter and sculptor, born to Apaches who had been imprisoned at Fort Sill

Vince Gill (b. 1957), country musician

Woody Guthrie (1912–1967), folk-singer, songwriter, and author of autobiography *Bound for Glory*

Wilma Mankiller (b. 1945), first female chief of the Cherokee Nation

Mickey Mantle (1931–1997), New York Yankees outfielder

Reba McEntire (b. 1955), country vocalist

Perle Mesta (1889–1975), Washington, D.C., hostess

N. Scott Momaday (b. 1934), Kiowa poet, novelist, and

painter; winner of the Pulitzer Prize for fiction

Bill Moyers (b. 1934), broadcast journalist

Chuck Norris (b. 1940), martial artist and actor

Brad Pitt (b. 1965), screen heart-throb

Wiley Post (1899–1935), aviator who made the first round-the-world solo flight

Lynn Riggs (1899–1954), play-wright

Will Rogers (1879–1935), humorist, actor, and writer

Little Jimmy Rushing (1903–1972), jazz pianist, violinist, and vocalist

Sequoyah (c. 1770–1843), Cherokee linguist and educator

Thomas P. Stafford (b. 1930), astronaut

Maria Tallchief (b. 1925), Native American dancer, prima ballerina with New York City Ballet

Jim Thorpe (1888–1953), Olympic gold medalist in decathlon

...and Great Places

Some interesting derivations of Oklahoma place names.

Antlers The town took its name from the Native American custom of nailing antlers to a tree to mark a good camping place.

Broken Arrow Named for a Muscogee (Creek) ceremony in which an arrow was broken to symbolize the reunion of two Civil War tribal factions.

Claremore Will Rogers called Claremore his home town, fearing no one could pronounce Oologah (*OOH-la-ga*), his nearby birthplace. Claremore was named for Osage chief Clermont.

Colony Originally called Seger's Colony, the town was founded by Indian agent John Seger, who established a model agricultural colony with 500 Cheyenne Arapaho in 1885.

Frisco Named by townspeople who mistakenly thought a railroad route under construction by the Oklahoma Central Railway was the Frisco Railroad.

Keota A Choctaw phrase meaning "fire gone out," in reference to a band of Choctaws who died of pneumonia.

Lone Wolf Named for Mama-daypte, a Kiowa chief.

Muskogee Site of an agency for the Five Civilized Tribes; until 1900, the official spelling was Muscogee, for the Muscogee (a.k.a. Creek) tribe.

Okeene Coined from the words Oklahoma, Cherokee, and Cheyenne.

Scullyville The original capital of the Choctaw Nation. The name comes from the Choctaw word for money, *iskuli*. Treaty-ordered government annuities were paid there.

Slapout Tiny town in the Panhandle, said to have been named for an early merchant who regularly answered requests for items with, "I'm slap out of that today."

Tishomingo Historic capital of the Chickasaw Nation, named for Chief Tishomingo, the tribe's last war chief. *Tishu* is the Chickasaw word for servant; *mingo* or *minko* means "king."

Tulsa Originally "Tulsey Town," the name comes from the Muscogee (Creek) word for town, *tallasi*.

Vamoosa Established in 1906 and named with a variation of the Spanish phrase for "move along." Everyone did, and the town disappeared.

Vinita Named for Vinnie Reame, sculptor of the Abraham Lincoln statue at the Capitol in Washington, D.C.

Glass Mountains The selenite-encrusted buttes in western Oklahoma appear on some old maps as "Gloss Mountains," perhaps due to the accent of an English engineer.

OKLAHOMA BY THE SEASONS
A Perennial Calendar of Events and Festivals

Here is a selective listing of events that take place each year in the months noted;
we suggest calling ahead to local chambers of commerce for dates and details.

January

Oklahoma City
International Finals Rodeo
International Professional Rodeo
Cowboy Association champion-
ships feature top competitors.

February

Oklahoma City
Winter Tales Storytelling Festival
Workshops and performances by
master storytellers.

Tulsa
Tulsa Indian Art Festival
Powwow and Native American
art show.

Watonga
Bitter Creek Frontier Daze
Living history reenactments
held in former Cheyenne winter
campground.

March

Corn
German Feast and Auction
Mennonite meal and auction of
handmade quilts, wooden toys,
and farm equipment.

Spiro
Vernal Equinox Walks
Archaeologist-led afternoon
and night walks discuss Spiro
Mounds culture.

April

Beaver
Cimarron Territory Celebration
The "World Cow Chip Throw-
ing Championship" is the highlight of week-long event.

Guthrie
89er Day Celebration
Chuck wagon feed, foot race, arts
and crafts show, parade, and rodeo
celebrate the 1889 Land Run.

Guymon
Pioneer Days and Rodeo
Free barbecue, trail rides, and
other events.

Muskogee
Azalea Festival
Blossoms fill Honor Heights Park;
parade, bicycle tour, craft fair.

Oklahoma City
Festival of the Arts
Fine arts, music, dance, and food.

May

Guthrie
Jazz Banjo Festival
Dixieland, ragtime, and big band
music on the four-string banjo.

*Oklahoma Cattleman's Association
Range Round-Up*
Working cowboys from 12 top
ranches compete.

Oklahoma City
*Chuck Wagon Gathering and
Children's Cowboy Festival*
Cooks from across the West meet
for food and entertainment at
National Cowboy Hall of Fame.

Pawnee
*Steam Threshing and
Gas Engine Show*
Demonstrations of vintage
farm equipment.

June

Norman
Jazz in June
Local, regional, and national
bands play jazz and blues.

Oklahoma City
*Red Earth Native American
Cultural Festival*
Tribes from Western U. S. and
Canada compete in Native
American dance competition, in
conjunction with art show and
other events.

Sapulpa
Route 66 Blowout
Classic car, truck, and motor-
cycle show, and statewide cruise
along Route 66.

Statewide
Juneteenth
Celebration of black culture.

July

Oklahoma City
Deep Deuce Jazz Festival
Local and regional bands celebrate city's 1920s jazz heritage.

Pawnee Fairgrounds
Pawnee Indian Homecoming and Powwow
Ceremonial feasts and dances in honor of veterans.

Terral
Watermelon Jubilee
Free melon, arts parade, and mule jumping contest.

August

Anadarko Fairgrounds
American Indian Exposition
Historical pageant, parade, dances, and greyhound and horse racing.

Freedom
Freedom Rodeo and Old-Cowhand Reunion
Open rodeo features nightly street dances and induction of annual "Old Cowhand."

Hugo
Grant's Bluegrass Festival
Oldest bluegrass festival west of the Mississippi River.

Konawa
All Night Gospel Sing

Tulsa
Jazz on Greenwood
Jazz, blues, zydeco, and other roots music on three stages in historic Greenwood area.

September

Apache
Fort Sill Apache Dance
Traditional Apache dance, plus horseshoe tournament.

Colony
Cheyenne and Arapaho Labor Day Powwow Celebration
Gourd dancing, competitive dancing, and art at local gallery.

Krebs
Ethnic Festival
Food stars in Italian celebration.

Oklahoma City
Oklahoma State Fair

Pawhuska
Bob Wills Texas Playboys Reunion
Former members of Bob Wills and the Texas Playboys perform.

Rentiesville
Dusk 'Til Dawn Blues Festival
Blues celebration at a vintage juke joint.

Tulsa
Bluegrass and Chili Festival
Bluegrass bands and Mid-America Regional Chili Cook-off.

Tuskahoma
Choctaw Nation Labor Day Festival
Homecoming of tribe includes address by Choctaw chief.

October

Cordell
Pumpkin Festival
Pumpkin pancake breakfast, arts show, "bullrama," street dance.

Guthrie
Oklahoma International Bluegrass Festival

Okmulgee
Council House Indian Art Market
Art competition and auction, powwow, and arts and crafts.

Wewoka
Sorghum Day Festival
Demonstrations of sorghum making, flint knapping, and hide tanning at Seminole Nation Museum.

November

Broken Bow
Beavers Bend Folk Festival and Craft Show
Turn-of-the-century arts, crafts, and music demonstrated.

Tulsa
Kids World: the Children's International Festival
Children learn about world cultures through hands-on activities, storytelling.

Festival of the Trees
Tulsa artists decorate trees and create gingerbread houses at Philbrook Art Museum.

December

Guthrie
Territorial Christmas Celebration
Historic district celebrates Victorian Christmas with home tours and a holiday ball.

Oklahoma City
Opening Night
New Year's celebration downtown

WHERE TO GO
Museums, Attractions, Gardens, and Other Arts Resources

Call for seasons and hours when open.

Museums

ATALOA ART LODGE
2229 Bacone Rd., Muskogee, 918-683-3281
A 20,000-piece collection of pottery, textiles, bead-work, and paintings.

BLACK KETTLE MUSEUM
Red Males and Broadway Sts., Cheyenne, 580-497-3929
Art and artifacts relating to 1863 Battle of the Washita and Southern Cheyenne culture.

CREEK COUNCIL HOUSE MUSEUM
106 W. 6th St., Okmulgee, 918-756-2324
Restored capital of the Muscogee (Creek) Nation holds peace medals, dance regalia, and other artifacts.

FENSTER MUSEUM OF JEWISH ART
1223 W. 17th Pl., Tulsa, 918-582-3732
Largest collection of Judaica in the Southwest.

FIVE CIVILIZED TRIBES MUSEUM
Agency Hill on Honor Heights Dr., Muskogee, 918-683-1701
1875 sandstone Union Agency holds art and artifacts from Cherokee, Seminole, Choctaw, Chickasaw, and (Muscogee) Creek tribes.

FORT SILL MUSEUM
437 Quanah Rd., Fort Sill, 580-442-5123
Original 1870s structures hold late 19th-century frontier military history, photographs, and items relating to Kiowa, Comanche, and Apache.

GILCREASE MUSEUM OF ART
1400 Gilcrease Museum Rd., Tulsa, 918-596-2700
One of the world's largest assemblages of art of the American West.

JACOBSON HOUSE
609 Chautauqua, Norman, 405-366-1667
Former home of art professor Oscar Jacobson, who brought Kiowa painters to world's attention. Now displays work by emerging Native American artists.

FRED JONES, JR. MUSEUM OF ART
410 W. Boyd, University of Oklahoma campus, Norman, 405-325-3272
Regional 20th-century painting, photography, textiles, and sculpture.

KIOWA TRIBAL MUSEUM
Hwy. 9 west of Carnegie, 580-654-2300
Holds 10 murals by Kiowa artists interpreting tribal history.

TOM MIX MUSEUM
721 N. Delaware, Dewey, 918-534-1555
Movies and memorabilia of cowboy silent screen star, a one-time Dewey deputy.

MUSEUM OF THE RED RIVER
812 Lincoln Rd., Idabel, 580-286-3616
Holds pre-Columbian and contemporary Native American artifacts from North and South America.

NATIONAL COWBOY HALL OF FAME AND WESTERN HERITAGE CENTER
1700 NE 63rd St., Oklahoma City, 405-478-2250
Art and artifacts representing 17 Western states.

NATIONAL HALL OF FAME FOR FAMOUS AMERICAN INDIANS
Hwy. 62 east of Anadarko, 405-247-5555
Outdoor sculpture garden with bronze busts of famous Native American figures.

OKLAHOMA CITY ART MUSEUM
3113 Pershing Blvd., Oklahoma State Fairgrounds, Oklahoma City, 405-946-4477
Five galleries and sculpture courtyard feature permanent and traveling galleries.

PAWNEE BILL MUSEUM AND RANCH
P.O. Box 493, Pawnee, 918-762-2513
1910 home and barn filled with memorabilia from Pawnee Bill's Wild West Show.

PHILBROOK MUSEUM OF ART
2727 S. Rockford Rd., Tulsa, 918-749-7941
Former home of oilman Waite Phillips holds collections of Italian Renaissance, Asian, African, Native American, and 20th-century American art.

PIONEER WOMAN STATUE AND MUSEUM
701 Monument Rd., Ponca City, 580-765-6108
Outdoor statue of Pioneer Woman; museum holds exhibits about women's lives on the prairie.

PONCA CITY CULTURAL CENTER AND MUSEUM
1000 E. Grand Ave., Ponca City, 580-767-0427
Memorabilia from 101 Ranch and Wild West show, Native American art.

SOUTHERN PLAINS INDIAN MUSEUM AND CRAFTS CENTER
715 E. Central, Anadarko, 405-247-6221
Showcases contemporary master craftspeople from nine Southern Plains tribes, plus historical displays.

STATE MUSEUM OF HISTORY
2100 N. Lincoln Blvd., Oklahoma City, 405-521-2491
Exhibits multicultural heritage, early settlement, Native American history.

WOOLAROC MUSEUM
Hwy. 123 southwest of Bartlesville, 918-336-0307
Oilman Frank Phillips's collection of Western and Native American art and artifacts.

Attractions

CHEROKEE HERITAGE CENTER
On Willis Rd., south of Hwy. 62, Tahlequah, 918-456-6007
Showcases art and history of Cherokee tribe; outdoor living history displays replicate life in 17th-century villages and Indian Territory settlements.

GUTHRIE HISTORIC DISTRICT
Downtown Guthrie, 405-282-1948
More than 400 blocks of turn-of-the-century commercial buildings and homes, featuring galleries, shops, restaurants, and bed and breakfast inns.

HARN HOMESTEAD AND 1889ER MUSEUM
313 NE 16th St., Oklahoma City, 405-235-4058
Barns, houses, orchards, and gardens paint a picture of life in Oklahoma Territory, 1890 to 1907.

MOHAWK LODGE TRADING POST
Hwy. 66 one mile east of Clinton, 580-323-2360
Oldest Indian trading post in Oklahoma displays and sells museum-quality beadwork, artifacts, and crafts.

OKLAHOMA JAZZ HALL OF FAME
322 N. Greenwood Ave., Tulsa, 918-582-1741
Honors Oklahoma's jazz and blues musicians.

OKLAHOMA ROUTE 66 MUSEUM
2229 Gary Blvd., Clinton, 580-323-7866
History and memorabilia of "The Mother Road" in Oklahoma.

PRICE TOWER
Sixth and Dewey, Bartlesville, 918-333-8558
Erected in 1956, the only Frank Lloyd Wright–designed skyscraper ever built.

WILL ROGERS MEMORIAL
1720 W. Will Rogers Blvd., Claremore, 918-341-0719
Holds memorabilia and photographs, theater, children's museum; graves of Rogers and family.

SPIRO MOUNDS ARCHAEOLOGICAL PARK
Hwy. 9 northeast of Spiro, 918-962-2062
Eleven earthen mounds served as religious center for
Mound Builders culture from A.D. 800 to 1450.

TALLGRASS PRAIRIE PRESERVE
17 miles north of Pawhuska, 918-287-4803
Bison graze on 37,000-acre tract of tallgrass prairie.

TUCKER TOWER
3310 S. Lake Murray Dr., Ardmore, 580-223-2109
Natural and cultural history exhibits housed in 1930s
governor's retreat built by WPA workers.

WICHITA MOUNTAINS WILDLIFE REFUGE
Hwys 115 and 62, Indiahoma, 580-429-3222
Bison, elk, and longhorn cattle range freely on
60,000-acre reserve.

WINDMILL MUSEUM
Hwy. 15 and U.S. Hwy. 283, Shattuck, 580-938-2818
Dozens of rare and restored windmills displayed in
outdoor park.

Homes and Gardens

T. B. FERGUSON HOUSE
519 N. Weigle, Watonga, 580-623-5069
The home of a territorial governor and newspaper
publisher novelist; Edna Ferber wrote portions of
Cimarron here.

GOVERNOR'S MANSION
820 NE 23rd St., Oklahoma City, 405-523-4367
The newly restored First Residence is a 1928 Dutch
Colonial, filled with antiques and Oklahoma history.

MARLAND ESTATE MANSION
901 Monument Rd., Ponca City, 580-767-0420
Oil baron's home features gold-leaf ceilings,
Waterford crystal chandelier.

MYRIAD BOTANICAL GARDENS AND CRYSTAL
BRIDGE TROPICAL CONSERVATORY
301 W. Reno, Oklahoma City, 405-297-3995
Translucent 75-foot-high cylinder filled with waterfalls and tropical plants, surrounded by 17-acre garden.

FRANK PHILLIPS MANSION
1107 Cherokee Ave., Bartlesville, 918-336-2491
1909 Greek Revival mansion and gardens.

SEQUOYAH'S HOME SITE
Hwy. 101 east of Sallisaw, 918-775-2413
Log cabin home of Cherokee linguist Sequoyah.

SOD HOUSE
Hwy. 8 south of Aline, 580-463-2441
Museum built around an original 1894 homesteader's
sod house.

TULSA GARDEN CENTER
2435 S. Peoria, Tulsa, 918-746-5125
Adjacent to the Municipal Rose Garden, a conservatory, and an arboretum, the garden center is housed
in an Italian Renaissance mansion.

Other Resources

STATE CAPITOL
2300 N. Lincoln, Oklahoma City, 405-521-3356
Series of murals illustrates settlement of Oklahoma.

WESTERN HISTORY COLLECTION
*Parrington Oval, University of Oklahoma, Norman,
405-325-3641*
Historical photographs, cowboys, Plains and
Southeast tribes, Native American portraits, frontier
settlement, journals of early explorers.

CREDITS

The authors have made every effort to reach copyright holders of text and owners of illustrations, and wish to thank those individuals and institutions that permitted the reprinting of text or the reproduction of works in their collections. Credits not listed in the captions are provided below. References are to page numbers; the designations a, b, and c indicate position of illustrations on pages.

Text

Michael H. Goldsen, Inc.: Excerpt from "Oklahoma Hills." Words and music by Jack and Woody Guthrie. Copyright © 1945 © Renewed 1973 by Michael H. Goldsen, Inc.

Levite of Apache: From *They Carried the Torch: The Story of Oklahoma's Pioneer Newspapers* by Mrs. Tom B. Ferguson. Copyright © 1937 by Elva Shantel Ferguson. Renewed © 1989 Levite of Apache. Reprinted with permission.

Penguin Putnam, Inc.: From *The Grapes of Wrath* by John Steinbeck. Copyright © 1939, 1967 by John Steinbeck. Excerpt from *The Mercy Seat* by Rilla Askew. Copyright © 1997 by Rilla Askew. Both, reprinted by permission of Viking, a division of Penguin Putnam, Inc.

Random House, Inc.: From *The Ancient Child* by N. Scott Momaday. Copyright © 1989 by N. Scott Momaday. Reprinted by permission of Doubleday, a division of Random House, Inc. Excerpt from *The Arapaho Way: A Memoir of An Indian Boyhood* by Carl Sweezy. Copyright © 1966 by Carl Sweezy. Reprinted by permission of Clarkson N. Potter, a division of Random House, Inc. Excerpt from *Shadow and Act* by Ralph Ellison. Copyright © 1964 by Ralph Ellison. Reprinted with permission.

Texas Christian University Press: James Auchiah quote from *Kiowa Voices: Ceremonial Dance, Ritual, and Song.* Copyright © 1981 by Texas Christian University Press. Used with permission.

University of Minnesota Press: From *The Day of the Cattleman* by Ernest Staples Osgood. Copyright © 1929 by Ernest Staples Osgood. Reprinted with permission.

University of New Mexico Press: From *The Way to Rainy Mountain* by N. Scott Momaday. Copyright © 1969 by N. Scott Momaday. Reprinted with permission.

University of Oklahoma Press: From Oklahoma: *Foot-loose and Fancy-free* by Angie Debo. Copyright © 1949, 1987 by University of Oklahoma Press, Norman. From *Wah'Kon-Tah: The Osage and the White Man's Road* by John Joseph Mathews. Copyright © 1932 by University of Oklahoma Press, Norman.

Williamson Music: Lyric excerpts of "Oklahoma" by Richard Rodgers and Oscar Hammerstein II. Copyright © 1943 by Williamson Music. Copyright renewed. International copyright secured. Reprinted by permission. All rights reserved.

Illustrations

AMERICA HURRAH ARCHIVE, NEW YORK: **13b** "Miss Oklahoma" by Earl Eyman, c. 1930s. Carved wood. 9" h.; **63a** Osage blanket/shawl, c. 1915. Wool and silk. 64 x 70"; RON ANDERSON: **84** *Car Scaffold Burial,* 1984. Outdoor sculpture/installation. Mercury Cougar with wood, cloth, glass, rawhide, feathers, mixed media; J. CACCIOLA GALLERIES, NEW YORK: **85a** *Bob White at Night* by Tom Palmore, 1998. Oil and acrylic on canvas. 24 x 30"; **85b** *Flying Fruit* by Otto Duecker, 1997. Oil on canvas. 42 x 42"; CORBIS: **86b** Cain's Ballroom. Photo Annie Griffiths Belt; JOHN ELK, III: **16** Longhorn cattle; **17b** Route 66 sign; **51a** *Holding the Claim* by Harold Holden, 1993. Bronze; **53a** Coca-Cola sign; **87c** "Golden Driller," 1966. 76' h; DAVID G. FITZGERALD AND ASSOCIATES, INC.: **50** Mural at Hominy; **53b** Victorian facades; **57** Shin'enKan; **62a** "Dorothy" chest by Kathy Kise Smith, 1998. Wood, paint, tile; **86c** Totem pole by Ed Galloway, built 1937–62. Concrete, reinforced steel, lead-based house paint. 60' h; GENERAL SWEENEY'S MUSEUM, REPUBLIC, MISSOURI: **33b** Cherokee Braves banner. Collection Dr. Thomas and Karen Sweeney; GILCREASE MUSEUM, TULSA: **15c** *Buffalo Bull* by W. R. Leigh, 1911. Bronze. 15' h. © 1956 by Mrs. Thomas Gilcrease; **22** *Crucified Land* by Alexander Hogue, 1939. Oil on canvas. 42 x 60"; **27** *U.S. Dragoons Meeting Comanches and Buffalo* by George Catlin, c. 1840s. Oil on canvas. 11¼ x 14¾"; **32** *Fort Gibson* by Vinson Lackey, c. 1950s. Oil on canvas. 9 x 12"; **36** *Longhorns Watering on a Cattle Drive* by Ila McAfee. Oil on canvas; MICHAEL HARDEMAN: **18, 19, 44, 48, 49a, 89** Gloss Mountains; ROBERT HUNT: **73a** Cover illustration from *The Outsiders* by S. E. Hinton; KELLY/MOONEY PHOTOGRAPHY: **42a, 51b** *Sacred Rain Arrow* by Allan Houser, 1988; **75a** Statue of Will Rogers by Jo Davidson, 1938. Bronze 7' h.; MIKE LARSEN: **11** *Flight of Spirit,* 1991. Acrylic on canvas. 22 x 11'. Courtesy the artist and the Oklahoma Arts Council;

LEWALLEN CONTEMPORARY, SANTA FE: **73b** *Preliminary Horse 3* by N. Scott Momaday, 1994. Monotype. 27 x 35"; LOS ANGELES COUNTY MUSEUM OF NATURAL HISTORY: **25b** Little Big Mouth and tipi. Photograph by Will Soule, c. 1870. Seaver Center for Western History Research; NATIONAL COWBOY HALL OF FAME, LIBRARY AND ARCHIVES, OKLAHOMA CITY: **70b** *Eagle Dancer* by Steven Mopope, c. 1930. Casein on paper. 10½ x 8". Siberman Collection. 97.07.089; NATIONAL GEOGRAPHIC SOCIETY IMAGE COLLECTION: **12a** Oklahoma flag. Illustration by Marilyn Dye Smith; **12b** Scissor-tailed flycatcher and mistletoe. Illustration by Robert E. Hynes; **26a, 69a;** NATIONAL MUSEUM OF THE AMERICAN INDIAN: **83b** *Shawnee Indians Having Cornbread Dance* by Earnest Spybuck, c. 1910. Watercolor on paper. 20 x 25"; OKLAHOMA HISTORICAL SOCIETY: **33a** *Self-Portrait* by Buffalo Meat, 1878. Pencil and crayon on ruled paper. 6¾ x 4⅜"; OKLAHOMA TODAY: **40a** *Shamrock* by James Gordley, c. 1975. Oil on canvas. 24 x 28". Private collection; OKLAHOMA TOURISM AND RECREATION DEPT.: **14a** Barite; **72a** *Angie Debo* by Charles Banks Wilson. Photo Fred W. Marvel; **87a** Blue Whale, built by Hugh S. Davis. 80' l.; **87b** National Route 66 Museum. All photos Fred W. Marvel; BEVERLY PARKER: **88** Garth Brooks. Courtesy Capitol Nashville; THE PHILBROOK MUSEUM OF ART, TULSA: **9** *Provisions* by Brenda Kennedy Grummer, 1976. Oil on paper. 18 x 18⅜". 1976.11.8; **21** *Prairie Fire* by Francis Blackbear Bosin, c. 1953. Watercolor on paper. 20¼ x 33⅛". 1953.7; **31** *Creek Women Cooking Fish* by Acee Blue Eagle, c. 1950. Watercolor on board. 18 x 28". 1950.10; **71** *One Sunday at Shawnee* by Brenda Kennedy Grummer, 1979. Oil on panel. 30 x 40". 1979.4.1; **82** *Return Home* by Virginia Stroud, c. 1970. Watercolor on board. 17⅞ x 30⅞". 1970.14; FRANK PHILLIPS FOUNDATION: **42b** Frank Phillips; PHILLIPS PETROLEUM COMPANY: **40b** Panorama of Burbank, Oklahoma, 1922; POTEET VICTORY GALLERY, SANTA FE: **5** *The Scarlet Heaven* by Poteet Victory, 1996. Oil on canvas. 48 x 72"; PRIVATE COLLECTION: **83** *Collector No. 5* by T. C. Cannon, 1975. Oil and acrylic on canvas. 80 x 72"; HOWARD ROBSON: **58** Villa Philbrook; SHEPHERD MANOR RETIREMENT CENTER: **66a** *Portrait of a Lady* by Nettie Shepherd, c. 1900–10. Oil on canvas. 24 x 20". Photo Julia Kirk; **66b** *Trees* by Nellie Shepherd, c. 1913. 11¼ x 8¼". Photo Wade Russell; **67** *Te Ata* by Nellie Shepherd, 1919–20. Oil on canvas. 40 x 31". Photo Wade Russell; SOUTHERN PLAINS INDIAN MUSEUM AND CRAFTS

CENTER, ANADARKO: **45a** Shaman's staff and longhouse prayer staff by James Watkins. Carved bois d'arc and cedar; TIM THOMPSON: **15b, 24a, 34** *Land Run* by Charles Banks Wilson, dedicated 1976. Mural. Acrylic. 15–25 x 7½'; **35b** *Pioneer Woman* by Bryant Baker, 1926. Cast bronze. 17' h; **52, 56b, 59a;** TIME-LIFE SYNDICATION: **75b** *Will Rogers Follies.* Photo Martha Swope © Time, Inc.; **76a** Katharine Sergava and Marc Platt in *Oklahoma!*, 1943. Photo Gjon Mili, Life Magazine © Time, Inc.; UNIVERSITY OF OKLAHOMA, OKLAHOMA MUSEUM OF NATURAL HISTORY: **24b** Incised bottle from the Spiro Mounds. Photo Pictures of Record; UNIVERSITY OF OKLAHOMA LIBRARY: **38** Cover of *101 Ranch Real Wild West Magazine*, c. 1911. Western History Collections; **45b** Quanah Parker. Western History Collections. Tilghman Collection; **54b** Campaign button. Carl Albert Center. Camp Collection; **56a** Oklahoma sod house, c. 1890s. Western History Collections; **69b** Bud Wilkinson, c. late 1940s. Western History Collections; USPS: **13a** *Oklahoma!* postage stamp. ® and © 1993 U.S. Postal Service. All rights reserved; VAGA, NEW YORK, NY: **54a** *Years of Dust* by Ben Shahn, 1936. © Estate of Ben Shahn. Photo The Granger Collection; WALKER CREATIVE, INC.: **26b** Thomas Nuttal; WB/UNIVERSAL/SHOOTING STAR INTERNATIONAL: **23a** *Twister* production photo. All rights reserved; WOOLAROC MUSEUM: **25a** Raccoon priests gorget. Photo Pictures of Record; **28** *The Trail of Tears* by Robert Lindneux, 1942; **59b** "Woolaroc" lodge

Acknowledgments

Walking Stick Press wishes to thank our project staff: Rose DeHeer, Miriam Lewis, Joanna Lynch, Thérèse Martin, Laurie Donaldson, Inga Lewin, Kristi Hein, and Mark Woodworth.

For other assistance with *Oklahoma*, we are especially grateful to: Laurel Anderson/Photosynthesis, Natalie Goldstein, Jan Hughes, Sandra Hilderbrand of the Gilcrease Museum, David Gabel of the Philbrook Museum of Art, Linda Stone Laws of the Woolaroc Museum, Aimée Downs at *Oklahoma Today*, Dave Crenshaw, David Fitzgerald, Michael Hardeman, Fred Marvel of the Oklahoma Tourism Department, Walker Creative, Inc., Christy Alcox and Tawny Corwin at the Office of the First Lady of Oklahoma, the Ackerman & McQueen Agency, and Kitty Pittman, librarian, Oklahoma Collection, at the Oklahoma Department of Libraries.